RETHINKING HIGH SCHOOL GRADUATION RATES AND TRENDS

Economic
Policy
Institute

About the Authors

Lawrence Mishel came to the Economic Policy Institute in 1987. As EPI's first research director and now president, he has played a significant role in building EPI's research capabilities and reputation. He is a labor market economist and holds a Ph.D. in economics from the University of Wisconsin. He is principal author of EPI's flagship publication, *The State of Working America,* which provides a comprehensive overview of the U.S. labor market and living standards. He is also one of the principal authors of *How Does Teacher Pay Compare? Methodological Challenges and Answers* and *The Charter School Dust-Up: Examining the Evidence on Enrollment and Achievement,* as well as a co-editor of *The Class Size Debate.*

Joydeep Roy joined the Economic Policy Institute after receiving his Ph.D. from Princeton University. His areas of research interest include the economics of education, education policy, and related fields in public and labor economics, including socio-economic segregation.

RETHINKING HIGH SCHOOL GRADUATION RATES AND TRENDS

Lawrence Mishel and Joydeep Roy

**Economic
Policy
Institute**

Other recent books from the Economic Policy Institute

The State of Working America 2004/2005
Lawrence Mishel, Jared Bernstein, & Sylivia Allegretto

Workers Skills and Job Requirements:
Is There a Mismatch?
Michael Handel

Losing Ground in Early Childhood Education
Declining Workforce Qualifications in an Expanding Industry, 1979-2004
Stephen Herzenberg, Mark Price, and David Bradley

The Charter School Dust-Up
Examining the Evidence on Enrollment and Achievement
Martin Carnoy, Rebecca Jacobsen, Lawrence Mishel & Richard Rothstein

Exceptional Returns
Economic, Fiscal, and Social Benefits
of Investment in Early Childhood Development
Robert G. Lynch

ECONOMIC POLICY INSTITUTE
1333 H Street, NW, Suite 300, East Tower
Washington, D.C. 20005

www.epi.org

ISBN: 1-932066-24-1

Table of contents

Acknowledgments

We are greatly appreciative for the data, advice, and comments we received from a variety of people. Of course, no one other than the authors is responsible for the product. Julie Yates at Bureau of Labor Statistics kindly provided some NLSY results. Census Bureau staff also provided information and data (Kurt Bauman, Greg Weyland, Carol Gunlicks). We also benefited from discussions with and information from NCES staff (Chris Chapman, Lee Hoffman, Jeffrey Owings, Tom Snyder, Marilyn Seastrom). Stephen Ruffini from American Council on Education provided GED data. Harry Holzer and Henry Chen provided tabulations of NLSY97 data. Cliff Adelman shared his knowledge of and tabulations from the NELS data. Our colleagues at EPI (Jin Dai, Danielle Gao, Yulia Fungard, and David Ratner) developed and tabulated data for us and helped prepare presentations. Russ Rumberger, Paul Barton, and Richard Rothstein provided a detailed review and many insights. We also received useful comments and information from Cynthia Lim, Leslie Scott, Bill Spriggs, Robert Balfanz, Daniel Losen, Arturo Vargas, Chris Swanson, Bella Rosenberg, Walt Haney, Rob Warren, Ed Croft, Elaine Allensworth, Eileen Foley, Martin Carnoy, Gary Orfield, Cyndi Holleman, Charles Kamasaki, Melissa Lazarin, Delia Pompa, Raul Gonzales, and Tom Mortenson. We also greatly appreciate the work of the EPI publications, policy, and communications departments, particularly Ellen Levy, Ross Eisenbrey, Nancy Coleman, and Stephaan Harris, for their work in preparing this report and doing outreach to the media. Last, Larry wishes to thank Alyce Anderson for her continuing support of all of his activities.

This report is part of EPI's education research program, which has received funding from the American Federation of Teachers, the National Education Association, the Spencer Foundation, the William and Flora Hewlett Foundation, the Metropolitan Life Foundation, and other contributors.

Introduction

Growing national attention has been paid of late to high school graduation rates in general, and the black-white and the Hispanic-white graduation gaps, in particular. This reflects a belief in the important role of education in a knowledge-driven economy, and an appreciation of the fact that those without at least a high school diploma will be more severely handicapped in their labor market prospects than those who have a diploma. The No Child Left Behind Act of 2002 includes on-time graduation as one of its important objectives.

Unfortunately, there is a lack of agreement on the magnitude of high school completion rates in the United States, as well as its trends over the last 10, 20, or 30 years. The status completion data, as reported by the Department of Education in the widely circulated *Digest of Education Statistics, The Condition of Education,* and other publications, show the percentages of members of various age groups who have completed high school and are based on household surveys (the Current Population Survey (CPS)) conducted by the Census Bureau. There are also household data showing the shares of the population in certain age ranges that have completed high school, college, and so on or have no degree whatsoever (effectively dropouts).

Several respected education policy analysts have severely criticized these "status completion rates" for allegedly overstating completion rates. Instead, several new measures of high school completion have been proposed, mostly based on administrative data on enrollment in public schools and diplomas awarded then reported to the Department of Education by state education agencies. These new measures show much lower graduation rates than the household surveys.[1]

This study reviews the available data on high school completion and dropout rates and their historical trends and finds that high school completion has been increasing and dropouts declining for over 40 years, though the improvements have been modest over the last 10 years or so. Unfortunately, we also find that some frequently cited statistics on high school completion that are based on the administrative and enrollment data mentioned above are seriously inaccurate. A recent National Governors Association taskforce report (2005, 9) cites these erroneous data, stating:

> [W]e know that about a third of our students are not graduating from high school....About three-fourths of white students graduate from high school, but only half of African American and Hispanic students do.

This statement reflects an increasingly used but incorrect characterization of the rate of high school graduation calculated from enrollment data reported by school districts and collected by the states and the federal government. This study finds that these analyses are contradicted by better data collected by the U.S. Department of Education that follow actual students' experiences and by the Census Bureau surveys of households. The new 'wisdom' —using enrollment and diploma data to measure graduation rates—exaggerates the extent of dropouts and fails to reflect the tremendous progress over the last 10, 20, or 40 years in increasing high school completion and in closing the black-white and the Hispanic-white graduation gaps.

We make no claim that our findings are novel—a leading expert on the measurement of high school completion and dropouts, Phillip Kaufman, came to many of the same conclusions over four years ago in a paper presented at the Harvard University Civil Rights Project Conference on Dropout Research in 2001 (Kaufman 2001).[2] Our study surveys what is known, and not known, about high school completion rates—both their current levels and the historical trends. This requires examining a range of data sources, including those based on school records, household surveys, and longitudinal tracking of students. To assess these data this study examines a wide array of measurement issues including: the extent of bias in household surveys from a limited sample (excluding the military, prison, and other institutional populations); the growth of high school completion by equivalency exams; and the bias arising from the inclusion of recent immigrants (most of whom were never enrolled in U.S. schools) in some measures. This study pays particular attention to the graduation rates of minorities in order to assess the claim that they have only a 50/50 chance of completing high school.

Among other things, our results suggest that, though it has significant biases, the Current Population Survey (CPS) provides a reasonable snapshot of educational attainment in the country and can be adjusted to provide trends in high school completion across different years. We find no reason to presume that the biases in the CPS are serious enough to render CPS data less accurate than administrative data. On the other hand, there have been few efforts by education policy analysts who rely on administrative data to investigate whether these data are themselves sufficiently accurate to support reliable conclusions about high school completion. We have also examined data from one state and two large cities that allow us to compare graduation rates based on student longitudinal data to the graduation rates used in this new wave of research: these analyses indicate that these new measures can be significantly inaccurate.

Our research finds that the conventional measures of high school completion computed from the school enrollment and diploma data are much lower than that of all of the other data and far below that of the very best data, i.e., the National Education Longitudinal Study (NELS). We also concluded that high school completion has grown significantly over the last 40 years and the black-white gap has shrunk significantly. Over the last 10 years, however, there has been little improvement, except among Hispanics. In particular, this study finds:

- The overall high school graduation rate with a *regular diploma* is between 80% and 83%, with the best data (NELS) showing an 82% rate. All of the household and longitudinal data sources show a higher graduation rate than the two-thirds rate computed using the school-based enrollment/diploma data.

- Estimates of the black rate of graduation from high school with a *regular diploma* range between 69% and 75%, with the NELS showing a 74% graduation rate. This is substantially higher than the frequently alleged 50% rate for blacks, reported from the school-based enrollment/diploma data. Moreover, the NELS data suggest that the alleged 50% dropout rate is double the actual dropout rate for blacks. In fact, the dropout rate for blacks is closer to 25% and roughly half of those obtain a GED, which allows entry into post-secondary education, the military, and other second-chance systems.

- Estimates of Hispanic high school graduation rates with a *regular diploma* range between 61% and 74%, with the NELS showing a 74% rate. This is substantially higher than the frequently alleged 50% rate for Hispanics reported from the school-based enrollment/ diploma data. Further, these data do not account for the additional 9% to 12% of Hispanics who receive a GED, which allows entry into post-secondary education, the military, and other second-chance systems.

- There remain substantial race/ethnic gaps in graduation rates with *regular diplomas*. Analysis of census data shows that in 2000, for those ages 25-29, there was a black-white gap of about 15 percentage points and a Hispanic-white gap of 23 percentage points.

- High school completion (either by diploma or GED) grew substantially from 1960 to the early to mid-1990s. This study looked at those aged 25-29 and found that in 1962 only 41.6% of blacks and 69.2% of whites completed high school, a 27.6 percentage point racial gap. By 1980 the racial gap had been cut by 63% to 10.3 percentage points, with both blacks and whites improving their graduation rates (to 86.9% for whites and to 76.6% for blacks). The racial gap was closed further to 6.0 percentage points by 1994 and to 5.0 percentage points by 2004.

- Trends in Hispanic graduation rates are difficult to track since it is important to be able to identify recent immigrants who were not enrolled in U.S. schools. This can be done with the data from 1994 and more recent years and the data reveal that the Hispanic completion rate (either by diploma or GED) has grown from 76% to 81.3% from 1994 to 2004.

- Increased incarceration of black men (and not any other race/gender group) leads some measures to overstate black high school completion and its growth over the last 10 years or so. Or, one could say that the increased graduation rates of non-institutionalized black men were offset by increased incarceration of other black men.

We find that the school-based enrollment/diploma data show an inaccurately low graduation rate, especially when diplomas are compared to ninth grade enrollment. This is because ninth-grade enrollment includes many students who have been retained as well as those entering ninth grade. This ninth-grade 'bulge' (counting those retained as well as those entering) has grown substantially over the last 10 and 20 years, leading to a wrong conclusion that graduation rates have fallen. School enrollment/diploma data, corrected for the bulge, show a steady graduation rate.

The results for minorities are especially biased since there are 23% more minorities in ninth grade than eighth grade. Simply comparing diplomas to the relevant eighth rather than ninth-grade class yields graduation rates for blacks of 61% and Hispanics of 64.5% rather than the 50% graduation rate frequently cited from the school-based enrollment/diploma data. Even with a correction for the ninth-grade bulge, these data yield graduation rates that are low relative to other, better data.

We were able to compare the various graduation rates (Swanson 2003 & 2004; Greene and Forster 2003; Greene and Winters 2005; Warren 2005; and Haney et al. 2004) computed with school enrollment data to the results from three studies using student longitudinal data drawn from the same school-based data. Our examination of data from the state of Florida and from New York City indicates that student longitudinal data show much *higher* graduation rates than those produced by the conventional school enrollment-based measures. This indicates that the computations that underlie the new conventional wisdom are seriously inaccurate.

We also compare the conventional school-based rate to those of a study that tracks Chicago students and shows graduation rates from 1996 to 2004 (Allensworth 2005). For some years the longitudinal data correspond to the conventional measures. However, the longitudinal data show steady progress (up eight percentage points), but the conventional measures show no progress for most of the period, indicating that these measures inaccurately portray trends.

There has been little examination of the procedures, consistency, and benchmarking of the school enrollment and diploma data, so it is hard to know why they produce such low estimates. However, if these data are incorrect at the national level and in the Florida, New York City, and Chicago case studies, then they should not be used for school district or state calculations. We may have to wait for data that track individuals to truly know graduation rates at the local level.

This study is organized as follows. Section I discusses in more detail the contradictions between the official graduation statistics and those estimated in recent studies, and why the issue is critical in any discussion about performance of U.S. high schools. Section II summarizes the information on graduation rates from the different longitudinal studies undertaken in the recent past by the Department of Education (DOE), as well as the Bureau of Labor Statistics (BLS). The rates of high school completion in these studies, which track individual students over time and sometimes include transcript verification of completion, are significantly higher than those estimated in recent studies. Section III discusses in detail the results from recent studies that use administrative data on enrollment and diplomas—data reported by the individual states to the DOE. Sections IV and V examine graduation rates estimated from household surveys conducted by the Census Bureau—the annual Current Population Surveys (CPS) and the decennial (2000) census. Section IV deals with graduation rates based on CPS. This is used by the DOE in its various publications but has been severely criticized recently. We analyze the various sources of bias in these CPS surveys and argue that many of these biases can be overcome by considering graduation rates from the 2000 census micro data (which we do in the next section) or the longitudinal studies referred to earlier. The microdata from the 2000 census, called the Integrated Public Use Microdata Series (IPUMS), allow us to calculate graduation rates for the institutionalized population and the military, which are excluded from the CPS sample frame, and to document the important role played by recent immigration in biasing graduation rates downward. These results are shown in Section V. In Section VI we discuss the historical trends in graduation rates, with particular emphasis on the graduation rates for minorities. Section VII analyzes the important role of the General Education Development certificate (GED) as an alternative way of completing high school, particularly among blacks and Hispanics. Finally, Section VIII brings all the different estimates together and compares them.

Appendix A briefly discusses the methodology and the sampling framework of the national longitudinal surveys discussed in the text. Appendix B discusses reports using longitudinal data from Florida, Chicago, and New York City. These allow us to compare measures of graduation rates proposed in the recent studies to much better estimates of graduation rates based on tracking of individual students through their high school years. Appendix C discusses the decennial census Integrated Public Use Microdata Series (IPUMS) data set in more detail and the methodology we use for calculating the graduation rate.

I. Motivation: The debate

There are large discrepancies between the official estimates of high school graduation as reported in DOE publications and unofficial estimates from recent studies that seem to suggest a dropout crisis in U.S. high schools. For example, the latest edition of the annual *The Condition of Education* reports that in 2003, 86.5% of 25- to 29-year-olds had completed high school, including those who received an alternative certificate (GED). Completions, defined in this way, include 93.7% for whites, 88.5% for blacks, and 61.7% for Hispanics. The *Condition* also shows that the completion rate has increased from 77.7% in 1971 to 86.5% in 2003, and that the black-white gap has considerably narrowed (from a gap of 23.0 percentage points in 1971 to a gap of 5.2 percentage points in 2003).[3]

However, a spate of recent studies has concluded that actual completion rates are much lower, particularly for minority groups. Greene and Forster (2003) argue that nationwide only 70% in the class of 2001 in public schools graduated with a regular diploma. They find that the graduation rates for minority students were particularly low—51% for African Americans and 52% for Hispanics. Similarly, employing a different methodology, Swanson (2004) finds that the national graduation rate is only 68%. Like Greene and Forster, he finds that students from historically disadvantaged minority groups (Native American, Hispanic, black) have little more than a 50/50 chance of finishing high school with a diploma.

There have also been concerns raised about the *trends* in high school performance. For example, Chaplin (2002) writes that, "By any measure, graduation rates have clearly stagnated if not fallen, and the degree ratio (number of high school diplomas awarded in a given year divided by the 17-year-old population) suggests that the stagnation began as early as 1970." Haney et al. (2004) find that the grade-eight-to-graduation rate increased only from 75% in 1979-80 to 78.4% in 1991-92, and thereafter fell steadily to 74.4% in 2000-01.

The main debate here is about the relative merit or accuracy of education statistics which are "official" to the extent they are all reported by the DOE. These statistics can be distinguished by the source of the underlying data:

- *Administrative data on enrollment and diplomas.* These data are based on what school districts report to their state departments of education that, in turn, compile them and report them to the federal Department of Education as part of the Common Core of Data (CCD) non-fiscal survey.

  Recently, some states and localities have been moving towards collecting longitudinal data on high school completion by tracking individual students over time. These longitudinal student data are drawn from the same underlying school data that yields the enrollment and diploma counts.

- *The Census Bureau household surveys.* The DOE uses the Census Bureau's estimates from the Current Population Survey (CPS) for its official publications on educational attainment. The CPS is a representative household-level survey that collects detailed information at the individual level. The CPS is the same survey used to measure unemployment each month and to track trends in poverty and income from year to year. Educational attainment data are collected every month, but the DOE reports the data from every March.[4] It is also possible to use the full amount (all 12 months) of CPS data as well as the Census Bureau's decennial census, as we do below, to examine trends in high school completion.

We also present high school completion and dropout rates drawn from a third type of data:

- *National Longitudinal Survey data.* The DOE has several longitudinal data surveys dating back to 1980 that follow students from either the sophomore year (High School and Beyond) or the eighth grade (National Education Longitudinal Study, NELS). The NELS is especially important data because student information on educational attainment was checked against actual transcripts. We also present some results from two other national longitudinal surveys conducted by the Bureau of Labor Statistics, namely the National Longitudinal Surveys of 1979 and 1997 (NLSY79 and NLSY97, respectively.)

A small wave of recent studies has criticized the CPS estimates of high school completion as being too high and unreliable. In addition to the papers noted earlier, these include Greene and Winters (2005), Sum et al. (2003), and Warren (2005). Most of these studies come up with their own estimates of high school graduation, primarily based on the CCD—the administrative data collected by the DOE[5]—and these estimates are much lower than the completion rates reported by the Census. It can fairly be said that these studies and the advocacy groups that have touted their results have established a new conventional wisdom on high school completion (as reflected in the NGA Task Force statement above) that only two-thirds of all students, and half of minority students, get a diploma.

The No Child Left Behind Act of 2001 (NCLB) and the trend toward accountability have amplified concerns over high school completion. As Barton (2004, 44) and Haney et al. (2004, 54) have noted, there are concerns that schools might trade off high school graduation rates for better test scores by having more poor-performing students drop out. Monitoring high school completion is a way to ensure this trade-off does not occur. Moreover, NCLB also mandates that states incorporate on-time graduation rates (with a regular diploma) in defining Annual Yearly Progress (AYP) objectives for their high schools.[6]

NCLB focuses on elementary and middle schools and seeks to improve their performance by implementing a regime of rigorous testing and accountability measures. Attention is increasingly being paid to the nation's high schools. In an oft-quoted remark in front of the country's governors, Bill Gates said in 2005 that the nation's high schools are "obsolete." A renewed push for high school reform has been given by the Bill and Melinda Gates Foundation, and several organizations like the Education Trust, the Harvard Civil Rights Project, and the Manhattan Institute have joined the issue. In light of these developments, it is imperative to have a rigorous discussion about the state of U.S. high schools—in particular, their effect on graduating students, especially minorities.

II. National longitudinal data

Over the last 30 years, the DOE and BLS have conducted different longitudinal studies of educational attainment, including high school completion. These include:

1. The National Longitudinal Study of the High School Class of 1972 (NLS-72), which consists of seniors in high school in the spring of 1972.

2. The High School and Beyond (HS&B) survey, which included two cohorts: the 1980 senior class and the 1980 sophomore class. Both cohorts were surveyed every two years through 1986, and the 1980 sophomore class was also surveyed again in 1992.

3. The National Education Longitudinal Study of 1988 (NELS:88), which started with the cohort of students who were in their eighth grade in the spring of 1988. These students have been surveyed every two years since that time.

4. The National Longitudinal Surveys (NLSY) program conducted by the Bureau of Labor Statistics, of which the NLSY79 and NLSY97 are important for our purposes. The NLSY79 consists of a nationally representative sample of 12,686 individuals who have participated in up to 21 hour-long interviews over the last 25 years. These individuals were 14 to 22 years old when they were first surveyed in 1979. The NLSY97 consists of a nationally representative sample of approximately 9,000 youths who were 12 to 16 years old as of

December 31, 1996. Round 1 of the survey took place in 1997, and these youths have been interviewed on an annual basis since then.

Longitudinal studies, which follow individual students over time, are the most appropriate forum for calculating high school graduation rates because they typically start with freshman or sophomore high school students[7] and follow them to their graduation and beyond. This makes it possible to calculate exact measures of high school completion, both on-time and final, unlike cross-section computations that either rely on successive cohorts or cannot suitably control for entry or exit of students from a particular cohort.[8] The most important disadvantage of longitudinal studies is that of ensuring the stability of the chosen sample—a problem referred to as attrition in the statistical literature. However, the studies referred to above have taken great care to minimize the problem of attrition, and it is widely accepted that this has very small effects on the final estimates (see Appendix A for more details).

We start by examining the results of the National Education Longitudinal Study (NELS:88) from the Department of Education.[9] It is the gold standard of data on high school completion because it tracks individual students' educational experiences and verifies them against actual transcripts independently obtained from schools. (See **Transcript Checking in the NELS** on page 15.) Equally important for our purposes, NELS:88 begins with students in the spring of their eighth grade and follows them through their high school years and beyond, allowing us to calculate the true high school completion rate. More detail on the NELS methodology and its sampling procedures is provided in Appendix A.

The NELS is a nationally representative sample of all regular public and private eighth-grade schools in the 50 states and District of Columbia in the 1987-88 school year. Because students were interviewed at regular intervals, the NELS allows assessments of educational progress both at normal graduation time, and two years and eight years after normal graduation time. These data on the class of 1992's educational attainment are presented in **Table 1.** They show that overall, 83% of students had graduated from high school with a regular diploma and another 7.7% had obtained a GED. Among blacks, 74.4% of students had a high school diploma—63.2% completed on time and almost all completed within two years after normal completion time—and another 13.6% had passed the general education development (GED) exam. So, by their

TRANSCRIPT CHECKING IN THE NELS[10]

One of the unique and most important features of the NELS:88 survey is that to provide reliable and objective indicators of educational outcomes, actual school transcripts were collected from sample members. Because transcripts were used to verify the educational attainment (i.e., graduation status) of a representative sample of the panel the NELS estimates of high school graduation are not subject to misreporting by respondents or their proxies.

The NELS:88 second follow-up in 1992 resurveyed students from the eighth-grade cohort, including students who were identified as dropouts in 1990, and identified and surveyed those additional students who left school after the first follow-up. In addition, the sample was freshened to allow trend comparisons with the senior cohorts that were studied in earlier longitudinal studies (NLS-72 and *High School and Beyond*).[11] In the fall of 1992, high school transcripts were collected for a representative subsample of students and all dropouts, dropouts in alternative programs, and early graduates.

Transcript data spanning the years of high school were collected for: 1) all students attending, in the spring of 1992, one of the second follow-up contextual schools;[12] 2) all dropouts and dropouts in alternative programs who had attended high school for a minimum of one term; 3) all early graduates, regardless of whether they attended one of the contextual schools; and 4) triple ineligibles enrolled in the twelfth grade in the spring of 1992, regardless of whether they attended a contextual school.[13] The transcript data collected from schools included student-level data and complete course-taking histories. Complete high school course-taking records were obtained for those transcript survey sample members who graduated by the end of the spring term of 1992; incomplete records were collected for sample members who had dropped out of school, had fallen behind the modal progression sequence, or were enrolled in a special education program requiring or allowing more than 12 years of schooling. *(cont.on page 16)*

TRANSCRIPT CHECKING IN THE NELS[10] *(cont.)*

A total of 2,258 schools were identified in the second follow-up tracing of the NELS:88 first follow-up sample; 1,500 of these were targeted for contextual data collection. All 1,030 schools identified as having four or more first follow-up sample members enrolled were included in the school-level sample with certainty (i.e., probability of 1.0). Schools with three or fewer students were subjected to sampling according to the following process. A random sample of 321 of the 1,008 (probability=0.31845) schools identified as containing one first follow-up sample member was selected for retention in the sample. A random sample of 104 of the 160 (probability = 0.65) schools containing two first follow-up sample members was selected for retention. Finally, a random sample of 45 of the 60 (probability=0.75) schools containing three sample members was selected. *Thus, because schools with more sample members were included with much higher probability, the large majority of sample members were included in the transcript survey.* [14] *Therefore the transcript checks provide us with enough confidence that high school completion rates calculated from the NELS reflect true underlying completion and are not sullied by untruthful reporting.*

eighth year after their "normal" graduation date, 88% of blacks in the class of 1992 were credentialed for college. Since 12% did not graduate high school or obtain a GED and another 13.6% did obtain a GED, the broadest possible definition of a black 'dropout'—not obtaining a 'diploma'—suggests a 25.6% dropout rate among blacks. So, our first conclusion is that the best data available show a dropout rate of about 25-26%, roughly half the size claimed by studies showing blacks have only a 50% chance of graduating with a diploma.[15] Similar is the case with Hispanics—66.1% obtained a regular diploma on time and another 7.6% obtained one within an additional two years.

    The National Longitudinal Survey of Youth, (NLSY79) also follows students over time, but unlike the NELS, does not check respondent answers against actual transcripts.[16] The NLSY data are shown in

TABLE 1   High school graduation rates: On-time, two and eight years later, NELS

	Regular diploma		Status in 2000 (age 26)			Final status
	1992	1994	Regular diploma	GED	Did not complete	Completion: Diploma or GED
By race/ ethnicity						
White	82.4%	84.9%	85.5%	6.7%	7.8%	92.2%
Black	63.2	73.5	74.4	13.6	12.0	88.0
Hispanic	66.1	72.4	73.7	9.4	16.9	83.1
Asian	93.4	94.7	95.0	1.3	3.7	96.3
All 1988 eighth graders	78.3%	82.2%	83.0%	7.7%	9.3%	90.7%

Source: Adelman (2006, Table L1) and personal correspondence with Adelman.

Table 2. The first column shows 'initial schooling' defined as the educational attainment when respondents first left school for at least *12 consecutive months*. Thus, if an individual dropped out of school but subsequently returned within a 12-month period to finish high school, he or she would be classified as a high school graduate (and not a dropout) in the first column. The second column shows the 'final' educational attainment as of 2002 for this cohort—a nationally representative sample of all youths born between 1961 and 1964 and living in the United States in 1979.

These longitudinal data show initial high school completion with regular diplomas at a rate of 84.4% overall and 77.6% for blacks and 70.6% for Hispanics. The data also point to the fact that some people attain a high school diploma or a GED after their initial experience in school, reminding us that 'on-time' educational status is not equivalent to the status of those in the workforce. The NLSY also shows a substantial share of students with GEDs, especially among minorities (roughly 10% among blacks and 12% among Hispanics). As with the NELS, these data show a much lower dropout rate for minorities (about 20%, including those with GEDs) than the 50% dropout rate claimed in some new studies using school enrollment data.

The NLSY97 consists of a nationally representative sample of approximately 9,000 youths who were 12 to 16 years old as of December

TABLE 2   Initial and final educational attainment, by race, NLSY79

	Degree when completed initial schooling (%)	Final educational attainment status (%)
All		
Less than a high school diploma	8.5	6.6
GED	6.5	7.2
High school graduates or more	84.4	85.6
White non-Hispanic		
Less than a high school diploma	7.0	5.5
GED	5.5	6.2
High school graduates or more	87.1	87.9
Black non-Hispanic		
Less than a high school diploma	12.2	9.1
GED	9.8	10.1
High school graduates or more	77.6	80.3
Hispanic or Latino		
Less than a high school diploma	17.8	14.4
GED	11.8	12.1
High school graduates or more	70.6	73.7

Notes: Initial schooling is defined as the time individuals first left school for 12 consecutive months.

Source: National Longitudinal Survey of Youth 1979.

31, 1996. Round one of the survey took place in 1997, and these youths have been interviewed on an annual basis since then.

A recent analysis (Hill and Holzer 2006) of the sample of 20-22 year olds from NLSY97, including the incarcerated, shows their high school completion status in 2002 and compares it to the comparable cohort in the NLSY79 for 1984. **Table 3** presents the data for both years by race and gender. It is striking how close the NLSY97 data are to that of NELS, with a high school graduation rate (excluding GEDs) of 82.2% overall and 74.5% for blacks and 76.4% for Hispanics. These data provide further confirmation that the new conventional estimates show *double* the minority dropout rate (or share not completing high school with a regular diploma) as other data (roughly 50% versus about 25%).

TABLE 3   Education status, ages 20-22 in 1984 and 2002, NLSY97

	High school diploma		GED		High school dropout		Completion: Diploma or GED	
	1984	2002	1984	2002	1984	2002	1984	2002
Total	78.9%	82.2%	4.3%	5.0%	16.8%	12.8%	83.2%	87.2%
White	81.4	85.1	3.9	4.9	14.7	10.0	85.3	90.0
Black	73.0	74.5	6.2	6.6	20.8	18.8	79.2	81.2
Hispanic	62.2	76.4	6.0	4.2	31.8	19.4	68.2	80.6
Male								
White	78.3%	82.8%	4.0%	6.3%	17.7%	10.9%	82.3%	89.1%
Black	68.4	68.3	7.3	8.3	24.3	23.4	75.7	76.6
Hispanic	55.8	74.7	8.8	5.1	35.4	20.2	64.6	79.8
Female								
White	84.8%	87.5%	3.7%	3.4%	11.5%	9.1%	88.5%	90.9%
Black	77.9	80.7	5.0	5.0	17.1	14.3	82.9	85.7
Hispanic	68.3	78.1	3.3	3.3	28.4	18.6	71.6	81.4

Source: Hill and Holzer 2006.

Table 3 also provides information on the trends in high school completion between 1984 and 2002. The overall completion rate, with a regular diploma, has risen from 78.9% to 82.2%. Graduation rates among whites grew 3.7 percentage points to 85.1%. Among Hispanics graduation grew 14.2 percentage points to 76.4%, a rise of 0.8 percentage points per year. Perhaps surprisingly, high school completion grew more among Hispanic men than women. Graduation rates edged up only slightly among blacks, reflecting no progress among black men and modest progress among black women.

Other longitudinal data can also be used to examine the extent to which high school completion rates have grown from the early 1980s to the early 1990s. For instance, the NELS data discussed above show higher rates of high school completion than those obtained in the earlier longitudinal study, called *High School and Beyond*[17] as shown in **Table 4,** which is reproduced from Kaufman et al (1996). These data show that dropout rates (measured as dropping out between sophomore and senior years, the most extensive comparison possible because the *High School and Beyond* data do not have information before the sophomore year) fell appreciably for every race/ethnic group

TABLE 4   Sophomore to senior dropout rates from the sophomore classes of 1980 (HS&B) and 1990 (NELS)

	1980 cohort (HS&B)	1990 cohort (NELS)
Race/ethnicity		
White, non-Hispanic	10.2%	5.0%
Black, non-Hispanic	13.5	7.9
Hispanic	19.2	12.1
Asian or Pacific Islander	1.8	4.2
Native American	26.9	17.0
Below poverty level		
Yes	14.5%	12.9%
No	7.0	3.9
Total	11.4%	6.2%

Note: Students who received an equivalent certificate (such as those awarded for passing the GED) were considered completers and not dropouts.

Source: Kaufman, McMillen, and Sweet 1996, Table 10.

between 1980 and 1990.[18] This study will examine evidence on changes in high school completion over the entire 1960 to 2004 period using CPS data.

III. Graduation rates using school enrollment and diploma data

The availability of NELS and other highly reliable longitudinal data discussed above raises the question of why the frequently cited graduation rates computed from the Common Core of Data (CCD)—enrollment and diploma data reported by school districts to their states—are so much lower. We make an extensive comparison of the graduation rates from the various data sources in section VIII.

We begin by discussing one of the prominent measures computed from these administrative data, the Cumulative Promotion Index (CPI) developed by Christopher Swanson at the Urban Institute.[19] The formula for calculating this measure, termed Swanson-UI from now on, for the class of 2001, say, is given by

$$Swanson - UI_{2001} = [\frac{E_{2002}^{10}}{E_{2001}^{9}}] * [\frac{E_{2002}^{11}}{E_{2001}^{10}}] * [\frac{E_{2002}^{12}}{E_{2001}^{11}}] * [\frac{G_{2001}}{E_{2001}^{12}}]$$

where E_{2001}^{9} is enrollment in grade nine at the beginning of 2000-01 school year, E_{2002}^{10} is similarly the enrollment in grade 10 in the 2001-02 school year, and so on. G_{2001} is the count of students who graduated with a regular high school diploma during the 2000-01 school year (Swanson 2004, 7).

The ninth-grade bulge

There are several reasons why graduation measures calculated by comparing enrollments to diploma may understate high school completion.

The most important one is that, although the measures are sometimes described as looking at how many entering ninth graders complete high school, the calculations do not rely on data on those entering ninth grade; rather, the only data available are the number of students enrolled in ninth grade. This is a crucial difference because many students are retained in ninth grade (partly in response to public outcry against "social promotions"): grade retention results in a substantial difference between the number of students *entering* ninth grade and the number *enrolled* in ninth grade. As **Figure A** shows, for the United States as a whole, there were 10% more students in public schools in ninth grade in 1987-88 than in the previous year's eighth grade,[20] and this figure steadily climbed upward to almost 14% in 2002-03.[21] This is a well-known phenomenon called the "ninth-grade bulge," which the Swanson-UI measure ignores.[22] The ninth-grade bulge is far greater for blacks and Hispanics[23] (e.g. in 1999-2000 there were 26% more ninth graders than previous year's eighth graders for each of these groups) as can be seen in Figure A.[24] Later in this study, we use CCD data to show how using ninth-grade enrollment instead of eighth-grade enrollment significantly biases downward high school completion rates (see Table 10).

If the growth of enrollment from eighth to ninth grade was taken into account—a large 'drop-in' rather than a 'drop-out'—the calculated graduation rates would be significantly higher. One can see how the ninth grade bulge distorts the results in the following example: 67 diplomas out of 100 enrolled in ninth grade yields a 67% graduation rate, but 67 diplomas out of 89 (100 less a 11% ninth-grade bulge) *entering* ninth graders is a 75% rate. Since the ninth-grade bulge is so large among minorities, the bias in calculated graduation rates is far greater. For instance, if one calculates a 50% graduation rate for blacks by comparing diplomas to ninth-grade enrollment, the presence of a 26% ninth-grade bulge indicates a diploma rate of 63%, far higher (though certainly an unacceptable outcome).

The Swanson-UI measure is not calculated based on a comparison of diplomas to the same cohort's earlier ninth-grade enrollment; nevertheless, the Swanson-UI is subject to the same distortions from grade retentions and resulting 'bulges'. These distortions generate dramatically wrong conclusions for minorities because of the 26% ninth-grade bulge. Moreover, because the ninth-grade bulge has been increasing over the last 16 years for which we have data (from a 9.5% bulge in the

FIGURE A **Ratio of 9th grade enrollment to previous year's 8th grade enrollment, 1988-2004**

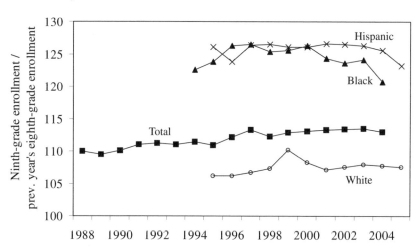

Note: The figures for individual races pertain only to the 40 states for which we have continuous data over this period, and are available only from 1992-93 onwards. The figure for "Total" includes all 50 states.

Source: Authors' calculations from CCD database.

1988 and 1989 school years to a more than 13.0% bulge in the last five years) there is a growing bias in completion rates measured with administrative data relying on ninth-grade enrollment as a proxy for 'entering' ninth graders, especially for minorities. Student retention in grades 10, 11, and 12 also distort the Swanson-UI measure.[25]

Warren (2005) provides actual data on ninth-grade retention in three states—Massachusetts, North Carolina, and Texas—in the last 10 years. These are shown in **Figure B**. In Massachusetts, the retention rate is less than 10% but it has been rising since the late 90s. In both North Carolina and Texas, retention rates have been well over 15% for most of the period. We do not have the breakdown by race, but retention rates for minorities are presumably much higher.

The fact that retentions are mostly concentrated in one grade, instead of being uniformly spread out across different grades, suggests that this is often a question of policy rather than actual school or student performance. In other words, a graduation measure using ninth-grade enrollment instead of the number of entering ninth graders in the de-

FIGURE B   Ninth-grade retention rates in selected states, 1995-2002

Source: Warren 2005, Table 2.

nominator may reflect school or district policy more than it reflects eventual graduation rates. *The fact that retention rates differ substantially across states means that the Swanson-UI measure distorts state-by-state comparisons.*

Using an eighth-grade rather than a ninth-grade enrollment base for calculations of graduation rates seems to be more accurate. One objection is that the computed rates do not reflect high school performance. That is true. Nevertheless, an important question is whether the calculation is more accurate. There are two biases when using an eighth-grade base. On the one hand, there is a slight influx of students transferring from private to public schools, which leads to an overstatement of completion (by not counting the transfers the base is too small). On the other hand, there is some dropping out that will occur between eighth and ninth grade, leading to an understatement of high school completion rates (which should be for diplomas earned by entering ninth graders). We have assessed the potential bias on inflation of public ninth-grade enrollment from private school transfers as being 3% overall and 4.4% for whites, 2.1% for blacks, and 0.8% for Hispanics.[26] The bias for minorities is smaller because they are less likely to be in private schools and the change between elementary and secondary school is smaller.

Thus, more of the ninth-grade bulge for whites can be accounted for by transfers (4.4 percentage points of the 7.5% bulge) whereas little of the 26% bulge for minorities can be accounted for by transfers. This suggests that the ninth-grade bulge, corrected for transfers, imparts an even greater distortion of the race/ethnic gaps in graduation than an uncorrected bulge. We have no way of assessing the dropout rate between eighth and ninth grade, so we do not know whether this bias offsets that of private school transfers. However, we suspect that there are as many or more dropouts than transfers among blacks and Hispanics: if so, then an eighth-grade base understates or does not bias graduation rates among blacks, but may overstate graduation rates for whites.

In a series of papers on the issue, Jay P. Greene and his co-authors at the Manhattan Institute have calculated another new measure of graduation rate. This is based on the CCD enrollment and diploma data, but is augmented by adjustments for the (estimated) increase in population between high school years, using data from the Census Bureau.[27] Greene's computations use a base of the average of the eighth, ninth, and tenth grades and, as shown below, are greatly affected by the ninth-grade bulge as well and by the retention in eighth and tenth grades. Greene's figures are very similar to those obtained by Swanson (2004) using his Swanson-UI measure. Swanson finds that the graduation rate for the public school class of 2001 is 68% overall and 75% for whites, 53% for Hispanics, and 50% for blacks—the Greene and Winters (2005) numbers for the graduating class of 2000 are 69%, 76%, 53%, and 55%, respectively.

Other researchers in the field have proposed their own measures. Miao and Haney (2004) survey the most important measures of graduation currently used and conclude that "this study found no evidence that the conceptually more complex methods yield more accurate or valid graduation rate estimates than the simpler methods." One of these complex methods is the Estimated Completion Ratio or ECR by Warren (2005). Warren argues, based on actual retention and grade-repetition data from Massachusetts, North Carolina, and Texas, that the best predictor of *entering* ninth graders in public schools in year x is the number of eighth graders in public schools in year x-1. He adjusts this number for migration by comparing "the total population of 17-year-olds—the modal age of fall twelfth graders—in a state on July 1 of one year to the total population of 13-year-olds—the modal age of fall eighth graders—in that state on July 1 four years earlier." The ECR shows a graduation rate of 71.9% in 2000, 71.1% in 2001 and 72.2% in 2002.[28] These alternative measures of high school completion are compared in section VIII.

Problems with administrative data

There appears to be some problems with administrative data but how much is hard to tell because there has not been much study of how these data are compiled or how consistent they are across states (Phelps 2005). It is clear, for instance, that the administrative data do not account for all diplomas. For instance, the administrative data were used for a study of California[29] even though the basic data are incomplete. Here is California's definition of what is reported by local school districts:

> ....the number of twelfth-grade graduates, by ethnicity, who received a diploma in the school year indicated or the summer following that year. It does not include students who took the California High School Proficiency Examination, programs administered by a community college, or adult education programs or who received a General Education Development certificate (GED).[30]

At best, the administrative data on diplomas reflect those given to students enrolled in K-12 schools in the prior fall. This will capture the vast majority of diplomas, but how many diplomas are provided (by entities other than regular K-12 school programs) to students in their late teens is unknown.

Different categories of high school completion

Some studies of high school completion across states, including data published by the NCES, can provide misleading comparisons because states categorize their types of completion differently. The CCD classifies all high school completers into three categories: Total Diploma Recipients, Total HS Equivalency Recipients, and Total Other HS Completers. The annual *Digest of Education Statistics* includes only the first category in its published number for Public High School Graduates. For the United States as a whole, the shares of completers in the second and third categories have been about 5-6% and 1.0-1.5% respectively since 1985-86. The second category consists mostly of GED recipients, though the numbers are not very reliable. It is important to note that the overall picture masks a lot of across-state heterogeneity. For example, while in states like Georgia, Oregon, and Alabama, the share of the third category (other high school completers—which includes those with certificate of attendance or certificate of completion) is more than 9% of all completers, in states like California, Illinois, and Massachusetts there are no completers in this category.[31] Therefore, it is important to include all types of high school completion (perhaps excluding the GEDs) when making comparisons across states.

It is evident that state policies have an important role to play in establishing different types of high school completion—the presence of alternate routes to high school graduation probably leads some students to complete via certification rather than regular diploma. It is also clear that the diploma counts from the Department of Education's CCD do not count all diplomas because they do not include diplomas awarded by educational institutions, such as adult schools or community colleges, which are not part of K-12 school systems, and maybe not even all 'on-time' diplomas. How much of a bias this generates and for which states and metropolitans areas is a fruitful area for future research.

Case studies based on longitudinal data from Florida, Chicago, and New York City

Another source of data on high school graduation is the longitudinal student data developed by school districts and states. States are beginning to compile longitudinal data systems that track students with unique identifiers so that student performance can be examined through 'value-added' assessment. These same data, with additional work to track 'leavers,' will increasingly be used to track graduation rates. The NGA report (2005) strongly urged states to compile longitudinal student data so that there can be better measurement of graduation.

The availability of such longitudinal data in a few places provides another opportunity for comparisons to new conventional measures. What is especially interesting about such comparisons is that they are drawn from the same underlying data on students from schools—the enrollment and diploma data used to compute graduation rates are based on the same student records that are developed into longitudinal data.

We were able to compare the various graduation rates (Swanson 2003, 2004; Greene and Forster 2003; Greene and Winters 2005; and

Warren 2005) computed with school enrollment data to the results from three studies using student longitudinal data drawn from the same school-based data. In particular, we have examined the new data from the state of Florida that was profiled by the NGA task force as a model for other states to follow. We also examined the longitudinal data that New York City has been providing for many years. Last, we draw on a new study of Chicago by Allensworth (2005).

Details of our analysis are presented in Appendix B. Our examination of data from the state of Florida and from New York City indicate that student longitudinal data show much *higher* graduation rates than those produced by the conventional school enrollment-based measures provided by the Greene and the Swanson-UI measures. This indicates that the measures that the new conventional wisdom relies on can be seriously inaccurate.

Our examination of the Chicago longitudinal data from 1996 to 2004 (Allensworth 2005) shows that for some years the longitudinal data graduation rates do correspond to the conventional measures. However, the longitudinal data show steady progress (up 8 percentage points), but the conventional measures show no progress for most of the period, indicating that these measures can inaccurately portray trends.

The characteristics and quality of student longitudinal data are not yet fully established. We have considered where longitudinal graduation rates may be biased because of a possible faulty characterization of some groups as 'leavers.' However, we have little doubt that any corrections to the methods of New York City and Florida would still show much higher graduation rates that the Swanson-UI and Greene measures. Thus, the available state and city longitudinal data provide an additional reason for skepticism about the accuracy and utility of the Swanson-UI and Greene measures.

IV. Census Bureau
Household Survey data

Data from household surveys such as the Current Population Survey (CPS)[32] and the decennial census provide other sources of information on high school completion rates. These data show higher rates of completion than the administrative data. However, several researchers have suggested that the rates of high school completion in the CPS are overstated (Orfield, Losen, Wald, and Swanson 2004; Swanson 2003; Sum et al. 2003). The reasons given for believing the CPS is biased include:

- a claim that self-reporting of educational attainment exaggerates completion because people exaggerate their own or their children's educational attainment;

- that the data exclude the prison population which has low completion rates;

- that there is underreporting/undersampling, particularly of minorities;

- that the CPS high school completion definition includes GEDs.

We are not aware of any systematic assessment of these biases that establishes their quantitative importance (Sum et al. (2003) goes the farthest). The following section discusses these biases and assesses their size and potential empirical strategies to account for these biases.

Pitfalls in relying on CPS for measures of educational attainment

The recent studies mentioned earlier have received widespread attention, both in the popular press and among policy makers, and have focused the debate on pitfalls of using CPS for measures of educational attainment of the population. The major points of contention are as follows.[33]

Self/proxy-reporting of educational attainment

The CPS, like most other surveys, relies on accurate answers from its respondents. This may lead to over-reporting of high school completion if there is a stigma attached to being labeled a dropout (respondents themselves or their parents may be ashamed of admitting to a third person that they or their children have not completed high school). As Greene and Winters (2005, 2) argue, "many respondents are probably unwilling to admit to a survey taker that they are high school dropouts." Sum et al. (2003, 6) also argue that October CPS estimates of high school dropouts are biased downward due to "biases in reporting of school dropouts by proxy respondents, especially the mothers of these dropouts."

This seems an important consideration and if true, might well lead to underestimates of the dropout rate. It should be noted that none of the critics have offered *any* evidence of a self-reporting bias, let alone a sizable bias. In fact, there are huge, longstanding empirical topics in economics—estimating the returns to education, understanding the growth of wage inequality—that rely on these household survey measures of educational attainment and never dwell on self-reporting bias.[34]

However, even if there is over-reporting of high school completion at any point in time, this will not necessarily bias the year-to-year trends unless people are becoming more or less truthful over time (i.e., the bias is growing or declining). Of course, there is no information available to assess any change in self-reporting bias.

The only data we are aware of that can address the self-reporting bias are the longitudinal studies conducted by the Department of Education (like NELS:88) that require transcript verification, so any non-truthful reporting is minimal. As Kaufman shows and as we argue below, the NELS transcript-verified graduation rates are similar to those obtained in household surveys, suggesting that there is no major self-reporting bias.[35] The NELS itself gives some idea as to the limited size of any possible self-reporting bias. Researchers looking at the correspondence between students' self-report and school transcripts created a special variable that reports the contradictions. This variable showed that in less than 5% of the cases do sample members' self-reports contradict school records—and even then the inconsistencies were not necessarily due to students lying about their educational attainment. Further, we have little reason to believe there has been a change in any self- or proxy-reporting bias that would affect our assessment of historical trends using the CPS.

Exclusion of all institutionalized populations and people in the military

The CPS, designed primarily for gathering information on labor market issues, only samples the civilian, non-institutional population. It excludes all people living in institutions (detention centers, juvenile homes, homes for teen mothers, hospitals, nursing homes, etc.) as well as people in the armed forces. There is concern that the educational attainment of these excluded sections of the population may not reflect that of the general populace. As Greene and Winters (2005, 3) argue, people in "prison or mental hospitals....house a disproportionate number of the nation's high school dropouts." However, people in the military generally have higher educational attainment—almost all of them are high school graduates—and this can potentially counterbalance the above bias, as acknowledged by Greene and Winters.

We tackle this problem by using micro-data from the 2000 decennial census, which has not been used previously in this debate. We use the 1% and 5% samples of the Integrated Public Use Microdata Series (IPUMS), which provides microdata from the decennial censuses for social and economic research. This dataset has the advantage of including institutionalized people and people in the military and is a representative sample of the U.S. resident population. This provides us with the educational attainment of people in the military and in institutions, which we can then combine to construct an overall measure of U.S. high school completion. As reported below, we find that the institutionalized population does have lower rates of high school completion, but the bias from excluding this population is offset by the additional exclusion of the military population, which has almost universal high school graduation. The exception is among black men where increased incarceration does lead the CPS to overstate high school completion and increasingly so over time as incarceration rates have risen. We adjust the CPS trends to account for this bias in section V.

Problem of under-reporting of certain populations which may have higher rates of dropout

Sum et al. (2003) point out that there is a problem of under-reporting (failure to obtain responses to the survey) of certain populations, particularly minority groups, in the CPS. A Census Bureau Web page[36] shows the coverage ratios for the 16-and-older population in the CPS, separately by race and sex, from September 2001 to September 2004.[37] Of particular concern is the low coverage of the CPS among young (ages 20-29) black men, where responses in early 1996 only represented 66% of the population—see U.S. Bureau of the Census (2002, Table 16-1)—with that for whites and Hispanics being higher, 84% and 75%, respectively. Coverage ratios for women are of much less concern, with coverage for young black women at 82% and that for whites and Hispanics at 92% and 90%, respectively. Coverage is likely to be somewhat higher for the 25-29-year age group that typically gets presented in studies of high school completion and which we analyze below. There has been no empirical examination of the bias due to low coverage for minority men in the CPS, but such research is sorely needed.

Sum et al. (2003) argue that because "men and women who are missed by the CPS survey are likely to be less well educated, the weighting process used by the U.S. Census Bureau to adjust for under-coverage rates will underestimate the true number of high school dropouts." The Census Bureau does adjust for such under-reporting by adjusting the population weights to reflect their assessment of the true population size (based on the Census and population estimates for later years).[38] The low coverage ratios in the CPS are a reasonable source of concern and need to be taken into account in any definitive assessment of trends using the CPS data (by looking at trends in coverage and hopefully finding a way to identify the impact of low coverage on completion by race/ethnicity).

This study will present results based on microdata from the recent decennial census, where the magnitude of under-coverage is much lower than in the CPS. Our computations of the decennial census data do yield high school completion rates below those of the CPS, 3 percentage points less among whites and 4 percentage points less among blacks. Nevertheless, estimates of high school graduation from the Census data are far higher than the estimates based on the CCD enrollment and diploma data.

We have also obtained from Census Bureau the CPS coverage ratios by gender and race for the 1994 to 2004 period, although we would have preferred to also have the breakdown by age, race, and gender. The trends in coverage give us some comfort that coverage ratios are not distorting the trends we analyze in this period. First, the coverage ratios for black men and women are comparable at the beginning and end of the period, suggesting that whatever bias there may be does not affect the endpoints in our analysis. Second, there was an improvement in coverage among blacks around the decennial census, with coverage rising from 1994 to 2000 and declining thereafter. We examined the high school completion rates for black men, both ages 20-24 (where coverage is known to be at its lowest) and ages 25-29. Changes in coverage would bias the data to show declining graduation rates in the late 1990s and improving graduation rates in recent years. Examination of the trends suggests that changes in coverage have not had any noticeable effect on the trends. We do not conclude that poor coverage is not a problem; however, it may be that the bias imparted by low coverage is not large enough to greatly distort the trends observed in the CPS, at least over the last 10 years or so.

Inability to distinguish between regular diploma holders and GED recipients

Another important point of contention involves the issue of General Educational Development (GED) certificates. A significant portion of high school students in the United States opt for GEDs instead of completing their regular diploma. There have been a number of studies over the last decade documenting the fact that a GED certificate is not equivalent to a regular high school diploma, either in its impact on post-secondary education or on labor market outcomes. However, the minimum cognitive content of a GED is higher than the average cognitive ability of a high school graduate. This suggests that dropouts who later achieve a GED are that sub-group of dropouts who were not failing academically but who could not adjust to high school or had other non-academic failures. High schools may have failed these students, but not in the academic way that most people think. They may have failed these students in non-academic areas. So most of the recent studies argue that GED holders should not be counted as high school graduates—at least, they should be documented separately. Greene and Winters (2005), in particular, argue that it is "inappropriate to count GED recipients as graduates in graduation rate calculations because doing so credits the very schools that failed to graduate these students with their successes. The primary reason we calculate graduation rates is to evaluate the performance of schools. But GED recipients are not truly "graduates" of any particular school. They are high school dropouts who later in life took it upon themselves to earn an alternative certificate."

Greene and Winters (2005), Greene and Forster (2003), Swanson (2004) and most of the other studies omit all GED recipients from their calculations of high school graduates. The first thing to note is that this approach is valid only if no student currently opting for GED would have completed high school in a world without GEDs. Since the presence of the GED process affects the costs and benefits of completing high school with a regular diploma, ignoring GEDs completely may not give us an adequate picture.[39] Second, the number of GED certificates being issued increased in the 1990s, and an increasing percentage of all GED certificates awarded are going to people aged 19 years or less. That is, GEDs are becoming more accessible, particularly to younger people, even though the academic content of the GED has gotten much tougher. Third, economic considerations (and more broadly, non-school factors) often play an important role in whether a student completes regular high school or obtains a GED—that is, opting out of high school to get a GED certificate may not always reflect the performance or effectiveness of schools. Section VII discusses the issue of GEDs in more detail, developing estimates of high school completion with regular diplomas (excluding GEDs) to make comparisons across data sources.

Important role of recent immigration

One important caveat in using the CPS measures of educational attainment for judging the performance of U.S. high schools is that these CPS measures at ages 25-29 include immigrants who came to the United States after high school age. With the influx of immigrants to the United

States in the last two decades, this is an important problem that can impart a serious bias to the estimates—both in levels and in trends. As we will see in the census microdata, almost half of Hispanics aged 25-29 immigrated during the prior 15 years. Perhaps more importantly, these recent Hispanic immigrants are much more educationally disadvantaged, compared to not only non-Hispanic whites and blacks, but also their counterparts in the United States. Because a meaningful calculation of high school graduation rates, used to evaluate the quality of the K-12 education system, should not include students who did not attend American high schools for a significant period of time, if at all, counting such students significantly biases downwards meaningful estimates of high school graduation. As we will show in the next section, the understatement of high school completion from the inclusion of recent immigrants is much larger than the overstatement from exclusion of the institutional population and the military (except for black men).[40]

V. Using the Integrated Public Use Microdata Series from the 2000 census to assess high school completion and potential biases in the CPS

The Integrated Public Use Microdata Series (IPUMS) consists of 37 high-precision samples of the American population drawn from 15 federal censuses and from the American Community Surveys of 2000-03.[41] These data contain detailed information on various aspects of individuals and households, including self and family demographics, educational attainment, work and income variables, disability, and migration status.[42] We use the 2000 IPUMS data, drawn from the 2000 decennial census. The microdata are available in two different samples—the 5% sample and the 1% sample. We use the 5% sample, because its larger size allows us to disaggregate variables much further, but results from the 1% sample are very similar.

The IPUMS microdata is important because, as it is census data, it covers the entire U.S. population—at least the resident part—and problems of under-reporting or coverage bias are much smaller. This study uses the IPUMS to generate estimates of educational attainment for the institutional population and for people in the military, and combines them with estimates for the rest (civilian, non-institutional population). Because the IPUMS has detailed data on the immigration status of individuals, including the year and country they emigrated from, we are also able to separately identify the educational attainment of 25- to 29-year-olds who have been in the United States for at least 15 years, and those who have been here for less than 15 years. Thus we are able to overcome, or at least significantly reduce, the problems in the CPS due to under-reporting of minority populations, exclusion of people in institutions and in armed forces, and inclusion of recent immigrants. We can also use these data to assess the size of the bias in the CPS from exclusions of the institutional and military populations and from the inclusion of recent immigrants. Technical details about our analysis of the IPUMS data are presented in Appendix C.

Overview of IPUMS results

Overall, there does not seem to be a big bias in using only the civilian non-institutional population for estimating educational attainment of the *entire* population. The bias in excluding the institutionalized population, which has much lower rates of high school completion, is neutralized by exclusion of people in the armed forces, who are almost all high school graduates. But across the different races there are important differences. Accounting for these two groups—the institutionalized population and the military—increases the percentage of high school completers for whites and Hispanics, but lowers the estimate for the blacks. The black-white gap in high school completion may be higher than the official statistics show.

However, it turns out that the largest bias in the CPS and in the decennial census data leads to an *understatement* of high school completion arising from the inclusion of recent immigrants in measures of educational attainment. Specifically, the tabulations of educational attainment for those aged 25 to 29 (which we and others focus on) that are presented by census and the DOE include people who immigrated in their teens or 20s. Yet, most of these recent immigrants were never enrolled in U.S. schools and their educational status does not reflect the performance of U.S. schools. We have calculated that the inclusion of recent immigrants leads to an understatement of high school completion by 4.0 percentage points. This is particularly important because this source of bias is growing over time and thus distorting any analysis of trends. It is also extremely important for assessing the educational status of Hispanics since more than half of the Hispanics ages 25 to 29 have immigrated in the last 15 years. The conventional measure which includes recent immigrants shows a high school completion rate for Hispanics of just 57.0%, but a measure excluding recent immigrants shows a 72.9% completion rate, 15.9 percentage points higher. There are also a growing number of black immigrants in their early 20s, both from Africa and from the Caribbean, which may affect measures for some cities but impart no bias in the aggregate.[43]

Discussion of detailed results[44]

Tables 5A-5C show the high school graduation rates for people ages 25-29 from the 2000 census both for the entire population and for the component institutional, military, and civilian non-institutional populations. The second row of each panel provides estimates for each population, which excludes recent immigrants from the sample. In particular, we exclude those who immigrated to the United States within the last 15 years because most of them were not in the United States during their high school years. Of those that were in the United States it is unlikely that their educational attainment reflects the few years, if any, that they spent in U.S. schools—it is much more likely to have been shaped by prior educational experience in their native countries. Our results are not sensitive to the particular choice of 15 years.[45]

The data in Tables 5A-5C allow us to assess the bias in high school completion from excluding institutions and the military from the sample. We can also calculate the bias from including recent immigrants in the calculations.

We find that the net bias in using the conventional CPS population of the non-institutional civilian population rather than the entire population (i.e., including the institutional population and the military) is minimal: the CPS noninstitutional civilian sample overstates high school completion by just 0.3 percentage points (0.5 percentage points when we exclude the recent immigrants) relative to a population that includes people in institutions, including prisons, and the military (see Table 5A). The bias from excluding certain populations is small because the inclusion of the less-educated prison population is mostly offset by the military population's high rates of completion. At the same time, the bias from including people who only recently came to the United States is quite large—4 percentage points (see the difference between the 83.8% completion rate in the total sample versus the higher, 87.8%, rate when recent immigrants are excluded). The net effect is that graduation rates are *understated* by 3.6 percentage points if, like in the CPS, we exclude people in institutions and in the armed forces but include all recent immigrants.

TABLE 5A Assessing the bias in graduation rates from excluding institutions and military and including recent immigrants, total

	Military	Institutional	Civilian non-institutional	Total	Bias from excluding institutions and military	Bias from excluding institutions and military and including immigrants
Total						
Including recent immigrants	98.5%	55.0%	84.1%	83.8%	0.3%	
Excluding recent immigrants	98.5	55.7	88.2	87.8	0.5	-3.6%
Non-Hispanic whites						
Including recent immigrants	98.5%	63.8%	91.3%	91.1%	0.1%	
Excluding recent immigrants	98.7	64.0	91.3	91.2	0.1	0.1%
Non-Hispanic blacks						
Including recent immigrants	99.2%	51.9%	83.1%	81.5%	1.6%	
Excluding recent immigrants	99.1	52.0	83.1	81.4	1.7	1.7%
Hispanics						
Including recent immigrants	96.5%	45.8%	56.9%	57.0%	-0.1%	
Excluding recent immigrants	95.8	47.9	73.4	72.9	0.6	-15.9%

Source: Authors' calculations from IPUMS 2000, 5% sample.

TABLE 5B Assessing the bias in graduation rates from excluding institutions and military and including recent immigrants, males only

	Military	Institutional	Civilian non-institutional	Total	Bias from excluding institutions and military	Bias from excluding institutions and military and including immigrants
Total						
Including recent immigrants	98.4%	54.9%	82.3%	81.5%	0.8%	
Excluding recent immigrants	98.4	55.6	87.1	86.0	1.0	-3.8%
Non-Hispanic whites						
Including recent immigrants	98.6%	63.9%	90.2%	90.0%	0.2%	
Excluding recent immigrants	98.6	64.1	90.2	90.0	0.2	0.2%
Non-Hispanic blacks						
Including recent immigrants	99.0%	52.0%	81.9%	78.8%	3.0%	
Excluding recent immigrants	98.9	52.1	81.8	78.7	3.1	3.2%
Hispanics						
Including recent immigrants	96.1%	45.7%	52.9%	53.1%	-0.2%	
Excluding recent immigrants	95.4	47.7	70.5	69.6	0.9	-16.7%

Source: Authors' calculations from IPUMS 2000, 5% sample.

TABLE 5C Assessing the bias in graduation rates from excluding institutions and military and including recent immigrants, females only

	Military	Institutional	Civilian non-institutional	Total	Bias from excluding institutions and military	Bias from excluding institutions and military and including immigrants
Total						
Including recent immigrants	99.0%	56.0%	85.9%	85.8%	0.1%	
Excluding recent immigrants	99.6	56.6	89.4	89.3	0.1	-3.3%
Non-Hispanic whites						
Including recent immigrants	98.3%	62.9%	92.3%	92.3%	0.0%	
Excluding recent immigrants	99.1	62.8	92.4	92.3	0.0	0.0%
Non-Hispanic blacks						
Including recent immigrants	100.0%	50.1%	84.0%	83.9%	0.1%	
Excluding recent immigrants	100.0	50.5	84.0	83.9	0.1	0.1%
Hispanics						
Including recent immigrants	100.0%	47.5%	61.5%	61.5%	0.0%	
Excluding recent immigrants	100.0	50.9	76.3	76.3	0.0	-14.8%

Source: Authors' calculations from IPUMS 2000, 5% sample.

For non-Hispanic whites, the bias from excluding the institutional population and people in the military is minimal; the same goes for inclusion of recent immigrants. For non-Hispanic blacks, the bias from including recent immigrants is close to zero. However, exclusion of people in institutions and in the military leads to an *over-estimate* of the black high school completion rate by about 1.7 percentage points. For Hispanics, just like for whites, bias from exclusion of institutional population and the military is small. However, there is a large bias from including recent immigrants, which *understates* the graduation rate by about 16 percentage points.

Tables 5B and 5C show these calculations for males and females separately. The net bias, from excluding institutions and the military and including recent immigrants, is larger for males than females—an under-estimate of the graduation rate by 3.8 and 3.3 percentage points, respectively. One interesting result concerns the graduation rates of black males. Exclusion of people in institutions significantly *overstates* black male high school completion—by slightly over 3 percentage points— primarily because of the significant share of this population that is incarcerated.[46] Note that there is no similar effect for black females, as Table 5C shows. Exclusion of the institutional population and people in the military does not impart any bias whatsoever, either to the overall estimates or to those for individual race/ethnic/gender groups.

Tables 6A-6C present estimates of the racial gaps in high school completion and assess the bias from including or excluding institutions, armed forces, and recent immigrants. The black-white gap for the civilian non-institutional population is about 8.2 percentage points, which increases to 9.6 if the institutional population and the armed forces are included. This increases marginally to 9.8 if recent immigrants, who for the blacks tend to be slightly more educated than the natives, are excluded. The net bias from including immigrants but excluding institutions and the military is to *understate* the black-white gap in high school completion in 2000 by 1.6 percentage points. Conversely, for the Hispanics, inclusion of people in institutions and in the armed forces only has marginal effects. However, inclusion of recent immigrants substantially biases Hispanic completion rates. Excluding recent immigrants and including the total population leads to a Hispanic-white gap in high school completion that is 18.3 percentage points (72.9% versus 91.2%) rather than the 34.4 percentage point gap found in the uncorrected data

TABLE 6A Estimating the graduation gap across racial groups, all persons (both genders)

	Civilian Non-institutional population	Total population	Total population excluding recent immigrants	Bias from Excluding institutions and military	Bias from Including recent immigrants	Net bias
Black-white gap						
White	91.3%	91.1%	91.2%	0.2	-0.1	0.1
Black	83.1	81.5	81.4	1.6	0.1	1.7
Gap	-8.2	-9.6	-9.8	1.4	0.2	1.6
Hispanic-white gap						
White	91.3%	91.1%	91.2%	0.2	-0.1	0.1
Hispanic	56.9	57.0	72.9	-0.1	-15.9	-16.0
Gap	-34.4	-34.1	-18.3	-0.3	-15.8	-16.1

Source: Authors' calculations from IPUMS (2000), 5% sample.

TABLE 6B   Estimating the graduation gap across racial groups, males only

	Civilian Non-institutional population	Total population	Total population excluding recent immigrants	Bias from		
				Excluding institutions and military	Including recent immigrants	Net bias
Black-white gap						
White	90.2%	90.0%	90.0%	0.2	0.0	0.2
Black	81.9	78.8	78.7	3.1	0.1	3.2
Gap	-8.3	-11.2	-11.3	2.9	0.1	3.0
Hispanic-white gap						
White	90.2%	90.0%	90.0%	0.2	0.0	0.2
Hispanic	52.9	53.1	69.6	-0.2	-16.5	-16.7
Gap	-37.3	-36.9	-20.4	-0.4	-16.5	-16.9

Source: Authors' calculations from IPUMS (2000), 5% sample.

TABLE 6C   Estimating the graduation gap across racial groups, females only

	Civilian Non-institutional population	Total population	Total population excluding recent immigrants	Bias from		
				Excluding institutions and military	Including recent immigrants	Net bias
Black-white gap						
White	92.3%	92.3%	92.3%	0.0	0.0	0.0
Black	84.0	83.9	83.9	0.1	0.0	0.1
Gap	-8.3	-8.4	-8.4	0.1	0.0	0.1
Hispanic-white gap						
White	92.3%	92.3%	92.3%	0.0	0.0	0.0
Hispanic	61.5	61.5	76.3	0.0	-14.8	-14.8
Gap	-30.8	-30.8	-16.0	0.0	-14.8	-14.8

Source: Authors' calculations from IPUMS (2000), 5% sample.

(for the civilian non-institutional population including all immigrants). Thus, the bias in the CPS from including recent immigrants nearly doubles the Hispanic-white gap in graduation.

Table 6B shows that the increase in the black-white gap from including people in institutions and in the military comes only from males, where it increases the gap from 8.3 percentage points to 11.2. There is no difference for females (Table 6C). For Hispanics, however, the large increase in graduation rates from excluding recent immigrants affects males and females more or less equally, though the bias is slightly larger for males.

Related points to note

Not all dropouts are between the eighth and twelfth grades. For the country as a whole, where slightly over 84% in the age-group 25-29 (including recent immigrants) report having a high school diploma or GED, about 1% report no schooling completed. Another 4% report dropping out in elementary and middle grades, so that the dropout rate in the high school grades (grades nine to 12) is just over 11%. If we further leave out people who report any of the six forms of disabilities,[47] high school completion rates slightly increases (from 84.2% to 86.2%).

Second, overall, and for each ethnic group, the female graduation rate is larger than the male graduation rate. The difference is lowest for the whites, at slightly more than 2 percentage points, but highest for the Hispanics, at over 8 percentage points. This declines somewhat (to less than 7 percentage points) when recent immigrants are excluded, implying that the gender gap for these new immigrants is even higher.

VI. Historical trends

Some of the discussions of recent high school completion and dropout rates claim a newly discovered crisis of low completion. Remarkably, these recent discussions have paid very little attention to the trends in high school completion over the last 40 years. In fact, historically there has been remarkable progress in raising both high school completion rates and in closing racial/ethnic gaps in high school completion. Historical trends can be computed from decennial census data or from the CPS, the only source of year-by-year data that goes back to the 1960s.

This study uses the published CPS data and computations of the CPS microdata to piece together the historical trends since the early 1960s. As discussed above, there are some important measurement issues that need to be addressed in using the CPS data. In particular, one must adjust, as we do below, for the increased incarceration among black men in the 1990s and for the increased immigrant population among Hispanics (which we can only do for data starting in 1994). In order to deal with these measurement issues we are forced to present the historical trends in three segments, 1962-80, 1979-1994, and 1994-2004. Issues regarding GEDs are reviewed in the next section.

Figure C shows the trend in high school completion (includes diplomas and GEDs) for blacks and whites from 1962 to 1980 for the population ages 25 to 29.[48] For this period, it is not possible to identify non-Hispanic from Hispanic whites and blacks so the racial categories necessarily include Hispanics. Also, since it is not possible to exclude recent immigrants from the data for this time period, we do not present the trends for Hispanics. Over the 1962-80 period, the high school

FIGURE C   High school completion by race, 1962-1980

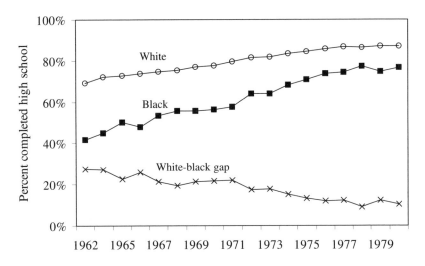

Source: Census Bureau tabulations of the March CPS.

completion rate improved remarkably among both blacks (up from 41.6% to 76.6%) and whites (up from 69.2% to 86.9%) and the black-white gap in completion decreased from 27.6 percentage points in 1962 to 10.3 percentage points in 1980.

Figure D presents the high school completion rates for non-Hispanic whites and non-Hispanic blacks for the 1979-2004 period computed from the monthly CPS data, which provides many more observations each year than the March CPS data used for the earlier period. High school completion among non-Hispanic blacks, ages 25-29, rose from around 76-78% in the 1979-81 period to around 88% in 2004, a rise of about 11.0 percentage points. Non-Hispanic white rates of high school completion rose by 3.8 percentage points to about 93.0% by 2004. Thus, the black-white gap in completion (by diploma or GED) narrowed about 5.0 percentage points from 1979 to 2004. We do not report the trends for Hispanics in this time period because we can not exclude the recent immigrants in the data before 1994. Further research should assess high school completion trends among Hispanics in this time period using the decennial census data for 1980 and 1990, which allows the identification of immigrants (unlike the CPS before 1994).

FIGURE D   High school completion by race, 1979-2004

Source: Authors' analysis of CPS data.

In **Figures E** and **F** we use our computations of the monthly CPS data to present trends for those ages 25-29 by gender/race from 1994 to 2004, excluding recent immigrants (those that have arrived within the last 15 years, a group whose educational attainment does not reflect the performance of U.S. schools). This is especially important for tracking trends among Hispanics—half of Hispanics ages 25-29 were not in the country 15 years earlier.[49]

Table 7 presents the data for the first and last years of this series and presents the changes over the period. Rates of high school completion rose for every race/ethnic/gender category. There was especially large progress in raising the Hispanic completion rates, up 4.2 and 5.6 percentage points among men and women, respectively. There were increases in high school completion among both non-Hispanic whites and blacks.[50] The increase in high school completion among black men of 4.1 percentage points reflects a sizable improvement at the beginning of the period, which happily is not because the first year is an outlier (data for the early 1990s accords with that for 1994). However, it is too early to tell whether the two-point improvement from 2003 to 2004 will hold up over time: consequently, we regard the 1994-2004

FIGURE E   High school completion rates by race/ethnicity for men, 1994-2004

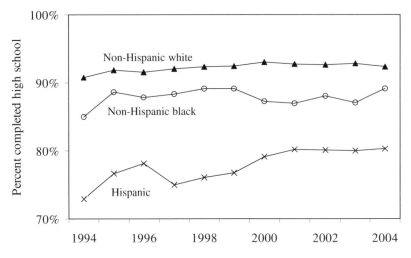

Source: Authors' analysis of CPS data.

FIGURE F   High school completion rates by race/ethnicity for women, 1994-2004

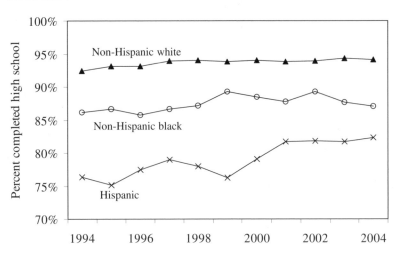

Source: Authors' analysis of CPS data.

TABLE 7 High school completion rates, 1994-2004

	1994	2004	Percentage-point change
Men			
Non-Hispanic white	90.7%	92.3%	1.6
Non-Hispanic black	85.0	89.1	4.1
Hispanic	72.9	80.3	7.4
Women			
Non-Hispanic white	92.4%	94.1%	1.7
Non-Hispanic black	86.2	87.1	0.9
Hispanic	76.4	82.3	5.9

Source: Authors' analysis of CPS data.

period as one of modest improvements in high school completion among black men.

These data do not, however, account for the incarceration of black men which, as discussed earlier, leads to an overstatement of high school completion in census data for 2000. The increased incarceration of black men (see **Figure G**) over the 1994-2004 period creates an upward bias (a growing overstatement) in the trends in completion for black men.[51]

Table 8 presents black male high school completion rates for the civilian non-institutional population (the CPS sample) and an estimate of high school completion for the population including the incarcerated—the civilian population.[52] The result is that incarceration biases the completion rate in each year (this overstates the bias in the CPS because we have omitted the military population) and the bias increases by 1.4 percentage points over the period. An analysis incorporating the effect of incarceration shows a more modest 2.6 percentage point improvement in black male completion rates rather than the 4.1 percentage point increase reported for the conventional CPS sample. Given that the 2.6 percentage point increase relies heavily on the improvement in the last year of the series (2003-04), we would consider that there was only a small or modest change over the 1994 to 2004 period. This would also suggest that the black-white gap in completion was relatively stable over this time period. Whether this failure to further close the black-white male gap in graduation was due to poor school performance or to a

FIGURE G   Share of black men, ages 25-29, in prison, 1994-2004

Source: Various publications of Office of Justice Programs, U.S. Department of Justice. See text for details.

change in criminal justice policy is something that other research will have to determine.

As we noted earlier, a definitive assessment of high school completion trends using the CPS requires careful attention to changes in coverage ratios (what share of the population subgroup actually responded to surveys) over time, especially for young black men. We do not claim to have made such an assessment in this report. Nevertheless, coverage ratios were extremely low in 1994 and 1995 because new methods of collecting the CPS data were introduced (U.S. Bureau of the Census 2002, Figure 16-1). Consequently, the coverage ratios in 2004 were not below those in 1994, the starting point of the last period we have analyzed. Therefore, we do not believe that changes in coverage ratios over the last 10 years have generated a bias in the CPS to overstate growth in high school completion among black men.

TABLE 8   Impact of rising prison population on black male measured high school completion rate, 1994-2004

	1994	2004	Percentage-point change
Civilian non-institutional	85.0%	89.1%	4.1
Civilian*	81.3	84.0	2.6
Bias from excluding prisoners	-3.7%	-5.1%	-1.4

* Includes estimate of prison population, but not other institutional populations.

Source: Authors' analysis of CPS and Bureau of Justice data.

VII. The General Education Development (GED) test issue

One issue in measuring or interpreting high school completion is whether and how to include those receiving a GED. We believe it is misleading to ignore GEDs in the discussion of how well disadvantaged students are performing and trends in high school completion, except perhaps in the narrower discussion of metrics for accountability under NCLB. How one counts GEDs in the overall education outcome discussion is worth debating: it does not seem debatable that GEDs shouldn't be ignored entirely.

First, GEDs provide a credential that facilitates further education: more than half the blacks or Hispanics that finish their original schooling with a GED go on to further education.[53] Although not many GED recipients complete a college degree, the years of post-secondary study they complete do raise their earnings.[54] Second, although GEDs do not have the market value of a regular high school diploma, they do allow recipients (even those without any post-secondary education) to earn more than high school dropouts.[55] Third, as GEDs became more accessible (those under age 21 were allowed to take the test, for instance), they became an alternative to a regular diploma. In turn, as GEDs became a partial substitute for a diploma, they affected the trend in diplomas. Thus, trends in GEDs and diplomas are not independent of each other (i.e., the increasing availability of the GED leads to fewer students obtaining a regular diploma). Fourth, it is hard to imagine having any 'second-chance' system, a critical component of any education and training system, without having some credential similar to a GED. This is another reason to not count GEDs as having no value. Finally, note that the minimum cognitive content of a GED is higher than the average cognitive ability of a high school graduate. This suggests that dropouts who later achieve a GED are that sub-group of dropouts who were not failing academically but could not adjust to high school or had other non-academic failures. High schools may have failed these students, but in non-academic areas.

At the same time, since GEDs are not valued in the labor market as highly as a regular diploma, it makes sense to track trends in both regular diplomas and GEDs. Consequently, this study develops estimates of high school completion that differentiate completion through a regular diploma or through a GED. One complicating factor in assessing the treatment of GEDs is that recent policy changes have made the test more rigorous and have led to fewer certificates being awarded; thus, the frequently cited empirical estimates of the labor market value of a GED that were done in the past may provide little guidance to the future.

Factoring in the GEDs into the historical trends

As discussed earlier, the high school completion rates measured in the census and CPS household surveys reflect both regular diplomas and GEDs. We have seen that there has been at least a modest improvement in high school completion according to this broader measure for every gender, and race/ethnicity group since the early or mid-1990s. The question we seek to answer in this section is how the growth of GEDs affects our conclusions about the *changes* in high school completion and how much is due to completion via a regular diploma versus an equivalency test.

We estimate the share of the 25-29 year old population with GEDs based on data provided by the American Council on Education (which administers the test) on GEDs granted each year by age. These data are shown in **Figure H**.[56] This share rose between 1.0 and 1.5 percentage points between the early 1990s and 2003, the last year for which there are data. We can use these estimates to assess how the extent of GEDs affects the trends in high school completion (presented above) and in turn, make comparisons of the *level* of high school completion in the varied data sets in the next section.

We now assess how the increased presence of GEDs affects our earlier assessments of trends in high school completion since 1994. Un-

FIGURE H   Share of population, ages 25-29, with GED, 1990-2003

Source: American Council on Education and Digest of Education Statistics 2004, Table 105.

fortunately, it is not possible to track changes in the share of the population ages 25-29 (or any other age range) obtaining a GED by demographic group: such data are needed to compute the high school diploma completion rates by gender and race/ethnicity.[57] We can, however, gauge the general trends over the last 10 years or so based on our estimates of the overall share of the population that has obtained a GED.

We estimate that the share of the population ages 25-29 with a GED has grown by about 1.5 percentage points between 1994 and 2003 and by a bit less (1.2 percentage points) between 1990 and 2003 (Figure H). If the relative rates of receiving GEDs by race/ethnicity in the NLSY and NELS have remained constant over this period, then we can extrapolate from the 1.2 to 1.5 percentage point increase in GEDs to the corresponding changes by race: a 1.0 to 1.3% increase among whites; a 1.9 to 2.3% increase among blacks; and a 1.7 to 2.1% increase among Hispanics. These data, in turn, suggest that the modest growth in high school completion among whites (see Table 7) over the last 10 years can be accounted for by increasing receipt of GEDs. The same can be said for both black women and black men (using the trend that incorporates the effect of increased incarceration). However, high school completion among Hispanics has grown far faster than can be explained by growing receipt of GEDs. In sum, it appears that the rate of completing high school with a regular diploma has been stable among non-Hispanic whites and blacks, and there have been continued improvements among Hispanic men and women.

VIII. Comparing alternative measures of high school completion

This section presents a direct comparison of nationwide high school completion by race/ethnicity in each of the three data sources discussed in the previous sections (school enrollment/diploma data, longitudinal surveys of students, and household surveys). The first focus is on those aged 25 to 29 in 2000 in CPS household surveys, which we can then match to our estimates from the decennial census.[58] We use a common breakdown of race/ethnicity into non-Hispanic whites, non-Hispanic blacks, and Hispanics and correct for higher incarceration among black men and the presence of recent immigrants among Hispanics. We also present separate estimates of high school completion by regular diploma and by GED. This yields an apples-to-apples comparison of the graduation rates (regular diploma or all completions, including GEDs) from various data sources, corrected for the biases that we have documented above.

We first accumulate all of the estimates of high school completion (regular diploma or GED) from both the longitudinal and household-based data for the year 2000 for those ages 25-29 (**Table 9**, top panel). The NLSY97 and NELS estimates are from the tables presented earlier as are the census data (these estimates exclude recent immigrants but include the institutional and military populations). The monthly CPS data are drawn from data presented above, which exclude recent immigrants. We have lowered the completion rate for blacks to reflect the incarceration rate of black men.[59] The March CPS data are drawn from tables published by the census for non-Hispanic whites and blacks: we have excluded Hispanics

TABLE 9 High school completion rates in longitudinal and household-based surveys

	Total	White	Black	Hispanic
High school completion (diploma or GED)				
NELS, 8th graders in spring 1988, status by 2000	90.7%	92.2%	88.0%	83.1%
NLSY97, 20-22 years old in 2002	87.2	90.9	81.2	80.6
Census, 2000, 25-29 year olds	87.8	91.2	81.4	72.9
CPS, 2000, 25-29 year olds				
*Monthly***	91.2	94.5	85.5	79.1
*March***	88.1	94.0	84.3	n.a.
High school completion by diploma				
NELS	83.0%	85.5%	74.4%	73.7%
NLSY97	82.2	85.1	74.5	76.4
Census	79.8	84.3	68.9	61.4
CPS				
*Monthly***	83.2	87.6	73.0	67.6
*March***	80.1	87.1	71.8	n.a.
High school completion by GED				
NELS	7.7%	6.7%	13.6%	9.4%
NLSY97	5.0	4.9	6.6	4.2
Census*	8.0	6.9	12.5	11.5
CPS				
*Monthly**	8.0	6.9	12.5	11.5
*March**	8.0	6.9	12.5	n.a.

*   Estimated based on the overall share of GEDs in the population and race/ethnic distributions of GEDs in the NELS and the NLSY (averaged).
** Black completion rate is lowered by 2.5% to correct for incarcerated male population.

Source: See Adelman (2006) for NELS and Hill & Holzer (2006) for NLSY97. The census and CPS numbers are based on authors' calculations.

because the March data include recent immigrants and would therefore be both incorrect and seriously different from the other data which all exclude recent immigrants. Again, we lowered the black completion rates in the March CPS for the greater incarceration rate of black men.

We also present the shares of the population with GEDs. For the NELS, these are drawn directly from data already presented from the survey. We have estimated the GED share for the household data (census and both CPS data sets) based on our estimate of an overall 8.0% GED share in 2000, and we developed shares by race/ethnicity based on the distribution of GEDs in the NLSY79 and NELS (averaged).[60] The rate of completion by regular diploma is then the high school completion rate less the GED rate.

The key results here are the comparisons of the rate of high school completion based on regular diplomas. The various data sets provide a range of estimates of the rate of high school completion with a regular diploma. The NELS completion rate, which we consider the best measurement, is 83%, somewhat higher than the two CPS or the census rates, which hover around 80%. The NLSY97 shows high school completion rates comparable to those in the NELS. The NELS completion rate for blacks is about 74%, which is higher than those found in the Census or the CPS. The regular diploma graduation rates for Hispanics are far higher in the NELS (about 74%) and the CPS (68%) than in the Census (61%). The estimates of completion by regular diploma are 79 to 83% overall, in the 84 to 85% range for whites, 69 to 74% range for blacks, and 61 to 75% for Hispanics.

These rates can be compared to those obtained from computations of school enrollment and diploma data from the Common Core Data (CCD), shown in **Table 10**. It is these CCD-based computations that provide the claim that minority students have only a 50% chance of graduating from high school and that only two-thirds of all students complete high school. The top panel presents the published numbers from Swanson's study (2004) using the Swanson-UI measure that are based on diplomas and the enrollment data for grades nine through 12, as discussed above.[61] The next panel presents Greene's published estimates of high school completion which are based on diplomas and enrollment data for grades eight through 10, and estimates of change in the total number of people in a cohort's population. These computations of graduation only count regular diplomas so the appropriate comparison is to the second panel in Table 9, which shows graduation rates with regular diplomas.

High school completion in the CCD-based estimates is far below those in the NELS, which we consider to be the 'gold standard' (because NELS data are verified by actual transcripts), particularly for minorities. The gap between the NELS and the CCD-based computations

TABLE 10   High school completion rates based on CCD school enrollment data

	Graduation rate			
	Total	White	Black	Hispanic
Swanson-Urban Institute (CPI)				
Class of 2001	68.0%	74.9%	50.2%	53.2%
Greene estimates				
Class of 1993	73.0%	——	——	——
Class of 1997	70.0	76.0%	54.0%	52.0%
Class of 2002	70.0	80.0	55.0	50.0
Swanson-Urban Institute (CPI)				
Class of 1994 (using 9th grade base)	71.1%	75.8%	52.6%	52.3%
Class of 1994 (using 8th grade base)	79.2	80.3	64.1	65.6
Difference	8.1	4.5	11.6	13.3
Basic completion ratios				
Diploma in 1997/9th grade enrollment, fall 1993	67.6%	76.0%	50.8%	53.1%
Diploma in 1997/8th grade enrollment, fall 1992	75.4	80.5	61.6	65.6
Difference	7.7	4.5	10.8	12.5
Estimated Completion Rates (Warren)				
Class of 1992	74.4%	——	——	——
Class of 2001	71.1	——	——	——

Note: 1992-93 is the first year with data on enrollment disaggregated by grade and race.

Source: The Swanson-UI numbers for 2001 are taken from Swanson (2004). The Greene estimates are taken from Greene and Winters (2005) while the Warren numbers are from Warren (2005). The Swanson-UI numbers for Class of 1993, as well as the Basic Completion Ratios, are based on authors' calculations using enrollment and diploma data from the CCD database. (A few states are omitted because of missing data.)

is about 10 to 14 percentage points (83% in NELS, 68 to 72% in the other data). For minorities, however, the gap is enormous, with Swanson-UI showing completion 24 percentage points lower than in the NELS for blacks and 20 percentage points lower for Hispanics. The gap between Greene's estimates and the NELS is just a few points less.

The CCD-based measures also report far less high school completion than in the other longitudinal survey, the NLSY, or in the household-based census, or in either CPS. Again, the differences are largest for minorities. The CCD-based high school completion rate for blacks is about 50%, with Greene's being as high as 56% in one year. In contrast, the census and CPS data show completion in the 69 to 73% range, *roughly 20 percentage points higher.* The gap between the CCD-based estimates for Hispanics—showing completion rates of 52 to 53%—is 8 to 20 percentage points less than that shown by the longitudinal or the household-based data.

We previously saw how the Greene and Swanson-UI measures were seriously inaccurate when compared to the level and trends of student longitudinal data generated by school records (the same underlying source for the enrollment and diploma data these measures rely upon). Now we see that these measures provide dramatically lower estimates of high school graduation than household surveys, including the census, and well-developed longitudinal surveys (NELS and NLSY).

One reason for the difference between the Swanson-UI measure and the other data is Swanson's failure to adjust for the ninth-grade bulge, as discussed in section III. To assess the bias from this, we present calculations from the national CCD data in the bottom panel of Table 10; specifically, we calculate the Swanson-UI extending back to ninth grade as Swanson does but also show a Swanson-UI extending back to eighth grade (which incorporates the growth of enrollment from eighth to ninth grade). We also present some simple ratios of diplomas relative to the eighth-grade enrollment (five years earlier) and relative to the ninth-grade enrollment (four years earlier).[62] Comparison of the Swanson-UI or the simple ratios with the alternative base years shows that the ninth-grade bulge biases these measures of high school completion down by 8 percentage points overall, by 11.5 percentage points for blacks, by 13.3 percentage points among Hispanics, and by a lesser 4.5 percentage points for whites. Nevertheless, even after correcting for the ninth-grade bulge there are still sizable gaps between the Swanson-UI measure and the NELS (as well as the other data sources)—a 5, 10, and 8 percentage-point gap for whites, blacks, and Hispanics, respectively. Therefore, even though the ninth-grade bulge imparts a very large distortion to the assessment of high school completion there still remains a large gap, especially for minorities between CCD-based measures and all other available measures.[63]

The Greene estimates of high school completion are also distorted by the ninth-grade bulge, although to a lesser extent. Greene's formula relies on the same numerator (diplomas) but uses the average of eighth, ninth, and tenth grade enrollment as a denominator.[64] Averaging these grades lessens the bulge, but it does not remove it: relative to a base of just eighth graders, Greene's formula has an overall ninth grade bulge of 4% and a bulge of 8% and 10%, for blacks and Hispanics, respectively. Greene's 'bulge,' however, is just a third of the bulge in the Swanson-UI measure of completion.

Warren argues that the ECR is validated by the fact that the ECR comes close to the graduation rate obtained from the NELS. Warren reports that for the class of 1992 the NELS gives an on-time completion rate of about 79.6% for public school students. The ECR, on the other hand, shows a graduation rate of 78.4% without the migration adjustment. However, this comparison is incorrect for at least two reasons. First, to make the ECR comparable to the NELS one has to exclude not only the migrants from the denominator, as Warren does, but also *the number of diplomas going to the migrants from the numerator.* We don't think there is a way of doing this from the published CCD statistics. If one only takes out migrants from the denominator but not the diplomas going to the migrants from the numerator, one is going to get an *overestimate* of the graduation rate.[65] Second, the NELS graduation rate (79.6%) to which Warren compares ECR is based on a comparison of the number of entering ninth graders to the number of diplomas awarded three years hence *to this cohort.* But the appropriate comparison is to the 83% graduation rate the NELS reports for 1994, when diplomas awarded in the two years past normal senior year are included. This more closely matches the ECR which is calculated to include *all diplomas awarded in a particular year* relative to the number of entering ninth graders three years ago.[66]

Since in any given year there will be some diplomas awarded to students who have taken more than four years to graduate, the ECR is not an on-time graduation rate. (One way to look at this is that this gives an estimate of the *eventual* completion rate, rather than the on-time completion rate, assuming that there are not any secular trends in the average number of years taken to complete high school.) In other words, to get the NELS-comparable figure for the ECR, we have to divide the number of diplomas awarded in 1992 *net of those going to graduates completing in more than four years* by public school enrollment in 1987-88. Warren, on the other hand, divides the total number of public high school graduates in 1992 (2,226,000, Digest of Education Statistics) into eighth-grade public school enrollment in the fall of 1987 (2,838,513, CCD) to arrive at the figure of 78.4%. This simple exercise highlights the fact that it is difficult to arrive at a conceptually correct estimate of graduation rates based on CCD enrollment and diploma data that will closely correspond to the NELS figure. The on-time completion rate in the NELS is significantly higher than *even the eventual completion rate* based on CCD data.[67] Warren's carefully constructed graduation rate still falls significantly short of the NELS figure by about 7 percentage points.

There are some definitional differences between the administrative and the other data, but these differences do not explain the large gap in estimated graduation rates with regular diplomas. For instance, the household-based and longitudinal data include both private and public schools, whereas the CCD data is for public schools alone. Given that private schools only comprise about 10% of enrollment, even if private schools have a 20-percentage-point better graduation rate (essentially graduating everybody!), then the longitudinal and household completion rates would be biased upward by just 2%—a bias that would mostly affect the rates for whites.[68] The longitudinal and household-based data also reflect educational attainment seven to 11 years after what would be the regular 'on-time' completion year. In contrast, the CCD probably reflects the receipt of regular diplomas of students who have been enrolled in school that same year. Thus, one difference between the two types of data is that the CCD probably doesn't capture high school completion past the ages of 18 or 19. Using the NLSY data as a guide (Table 2), the 'late' completion among blacks and Hispanics is roughly three percentage points and among whites about 1 percentage point. Again, this still leaves a nontrivial gap between the CCD-based measures and all of the other sources of data.

It is difficult to assess what can be causing these gaps because there is very little documentation and assessment of the CCD data that we could locate, especially since the measures are not necessarily consistent across states. This lack of information is why we hedge our conclusions above when discussing the characteristics of the CCD. This lack of information about the CCD has also left us puzzled as to why analysts give such great confidence to their calculations using the CCD data.[69]

Conclusion

Regarding measurement, our conclusion is that the best data—the longitudinal data, especially the NELS—is corroborated by the census surveys, especially the decennial census, which show that measures of high school completion based on the CCD enrollment/diploma data are too low and are the 'outliers.' As we noted in the introduction, a leading expert on the measurement of high school completion and dropouts, Phillip Kaufman, came to the same conclusions in 2001. In particular, we find that the frequently cited statistics that claim blacks have only a 50/50 chance of graduating from high school are seriously inaccurate both because of the failure to adjust for the ninth-grade bulge and becasue their use of the CCD data. The facts are that about 25% of black students drop out and half of those dropouts obtain a GED.

Finding that about 75% of blacks complete high school with a regular diploma rather than just 50% is more encouraging but not satisfying since that still leaves a sizable portion of blacks without a regular diploma. Correspondingly, finding that the black-white gap in graduation has been dramatically reduced over the last 40 years is encouraging but not satisfying since there has been little further progress over the last 10 years. It is important to note that a large percentage of blacks complete high school through the GED, which facilitates access to post-secondary education and higher earnings. However, it is undoubtedly the case that it would be more advantageous for these students to obtain a regular diploma rather than a GED. It is also disappointing to report that less than 40% of 13-year-old black men attain a diploma in the Chicago public schools by the time they are 19.

One of our important findings is that progress in improving the graduation rate among Hispanics has been obscured by the inclusion of recent immigrants (most of who were never enrolled in U.S. schools) in published measures based on household data. Yet, there still remains a large gap in high school completion between Hispanics and whites.

In sum, it is important to both accurately assess the scale of the high school dropout problem and to acknowledge the extensive progress that has been made. However, any policy assessment of properly measured high school completion rates would indicate much further room for improvement, particularly for minorities.

Our research does not address directly another important aspect of the concern for tracking high school completion—the desire to hold schools and school districts accountable. Unfortunately, the only data available at the school district level are the CCD data that we judge to provide inaccurate estimates of high school completion. This suggests that measures of high school completion at the school-district level will probably have to wait until data systems that track individual students are available. We must admit that developing longitudinal data systems in each state may not yield authoritative estimates of graduation. This is because it is necessary to be able to track down and categorize all of the students who leave the system and determine whether they have transferred to another school or have abandoned their education. Doing so will require a national system and sufficient resources for schools to track 'leavers'. We are skeptical that this will happen anytime in the near future.

In this, as in all research topics, it is possible to urge further research. In this case we feel even more strongly that more research is needed. In particular, there needs to be a much greater understanding of how the CCD is compiled and what it measures, including the consistency across states. Understanding the historical trends in Hispanic high school completion requires data that allow one to exclude recent immigrants, a motivation to develop a historical series based on the decennial censuses. Assessing the bias, now and in the past, in the CPS due to low coverage ratios also is critically important. Last, a more complete understanding of the role that the GED has played and currently plays in our second-chance systems would also be a useful addition to the current discussion.

APPENDIX A
National longitudinal studies

The ideal way to calculate graduation rates would be to follow individual students over time, as they enter high school and progress through it. This would obviate the need to rely on survey data like the CPS or other administrative data which have several pitfalls. Unfortunately, such universal tracking of high school students is resource-intensive and is not currently practiced. However, the Department of Education and other entities often embark on longitudinal studies, where they follow representative groups of students over time. There have been at least three important longitudinal surveys of high school students over the last 25 years, namely the National Longitudinal Survey of Youth (NLSY), since 1979, the High School and Beyond Survey (HS&B), since 1980, and the National Educational Longitudinal Study (NELS), since 1988. The HS&B and NELS surveys, particularly NELS, are directly relevant to the issues of high school graduation and dropout and provide important evidence.[70] This appendix provides a brief description of the surveys and discusses whether the sampling framework and attrition[71] could have significantly biased their results.

Brief description of the surveys
National Longitudinal Survey of Youth (NLSY), 1979
The NLSY79 is a nationally representative sample of 12,686 young men and women who were 14-22 years old when they were first surveyed in 1979. Since then, these individuals have been interviewed annually through 1994 and are currently interviewed on a biennial basis. The NLSY data are invaluable as they "provide researchers an opportunity to study a large sample that represents American men and women born in the 1950s and 1960s, and living in the United States in 1979."[72]

Although a primary focus of the NLSY79 survey is labor force behavior, the survey contains a broad set of questions including detailed questions on educational attainment. It also includes an aptitude measure, a school survey, and high school transcript information.[73]

High School and Beyond (HS&B), since 1980
The HS&B survey included two cohorts: the 1980 senior class, and the 1980 sophomore class. Both cohorts were surveyed every two years through 1986, and the 1980 sophomore class was also surveyed again in 1992. The sampling frame was a two-stage stratified sample where 1,100 schools were selected in the first stage and 36 students were selected randomly from each school in the second stage. For the HS&B second follow-up study, which is used for calculations reported below, the overall unweighted student response rate was about 94%.

National Educational Longitudinal Study (NELS:88), since 1988[74]
The NELS:88 baseline sample was made up of a national probability sample of all regular public and private eighth-grade schools in the 50 states and District of Columbia in the 1987-88 school year.[75] It started out with 1,057 schools, usable student data were received for 1,052 of the schools. The total eighth-grade enrollment for these 1,052 NELS:88 sample schools was 202,996. During the listing procedures (before 24-26 students were selected per school), 5.35% of the students were excluded because they were identified by school staff as being incapable of completing the NELS:88 instruments owing to limitations in their language proficiency or to mental or physical disabilities. Ultimately, 93%, or 24,599, of the sample students participated in the base year survey in the spring of 1988.

In the base year, about 5.35% of the students were excluded because they were identified by school staff as being incapable of completing the survey instruments, due to limitations in their language proficiency or to mental or physical disabilities. However, a special study was initiated during the NELS:88 first follow-up survey, conducted in the spring of 1990, to identify the enrollment status of a representative sample of the base year ineligible students. This was done because the characteristics and educational outcomes of the students excluded from the base year might differ from those of students who participated in the base year data collection. Data from this sample were then combined with first and second follow-up data in order to compute eighth-through-tenth-grade, tenth-through-twelfth-grade, and eighth-through-twelfth-grade cohort dropout rates. (See Kaufman et al. 1999, 78-80.)[76]

The NELS:88 first follow-up survey was conducted in the spring of 1990, covering students, dropouts, teachers, and school administrators, with a successful data collection effort for approximately 93% of the base-year student respondents. In addition, as just mentioned, a special study was done for a representative sample of students who were ineligible in the base year.

The second follow-up survey was conducted in the spring of 1992. Approximately 91% of the sample of students participated in the second follow-up survey[77] (un-weighted response rate was 94%), with 88% of the dropouts responding.

The second follow-up High School Transcript Study was conducted in the fall of 1992. The transcript data collected from schools included student-level data (e.g., number of days absent per school year, standardized test scores) and complete course-taking histories. Complete high school course-taking records were obtained only for those transcript survey sample members who had graduated by the end of the 1992 spring term; incomplete records were collected for sample members who had dropped out of school, had fallen behind the modal progression sequence, or were enrolled in a special education program requiring or allowing more than 12 years of schooling. Student coverage rates were 89.5% for the total transcript sample and 74.2% for the dropout/alternative completers. See the box on page 15 in section II for more details on transcript verification in the NELS.

The basic NELS:88 procedure for identifying a dropout[78] was to confirm school-reported dropout status with the student's household. For the first follow-up, dropout status was obtained first from the school and then confirmed with the household for 96.4% of the dropouts. Thus, only 3.6% of the dropouts were identified by only school-reported information. For the second follow-up, 4.9% of the dropouts were identified by only school-reported information.

The 1988-90 dropout rate requires data from both 1988 and 1990. As a result, the size of the sample used in computing the 1988-90 rate is tied to the size of the sample in 1990. Many students changed schools between 1988 and 1990. Because of the costs associated with following small numbers of students in many schools, a subsampling operation was conducted at the time of the first follow-up. Of the 24,599 students who participated in 1988, 20,263 students were sampled, and 130 were found to be out of scope (due to death or migration out of the country). The dropout rates from 1988 to 1990 reflect the experiences of 20,133 sample cases. Some 1,088 sample cases dropped out, and 19,045 sample cases continued in school.

The 1990–92 rate starts from the 19,045 student sample cases. Some 91 of the student sample cases from 1990 were identified as out of scope in 1992. The dropout rates from 1990 to 1992 reflect the experiences of 18,954 student sample cases.

The 1988–92 rates reflect the experiences of the 20,070 student sample cases. These cases result from the 20,263 subsampled student cases in 1990; less the 92 cases that were out of scope in both 1990 and 1992, less the 91 student sample cases identified as out of scope in 1992, less the 10 dropout sample cases identified as out of scope in 1992. Note that 24 student sample cases who were out of the country in 1990 returned to school in the United States by spring 1992, and an additional 14 student sample cases who were out of the country in spring 1990 returned to the United States by spring 1992 but did not re-enroll (dropouts). In addition, another 354 student sample cases who dropped out between 1988 and 1990 returned to school by spring 1992.

Problem of attrition in these longitudinal studies

Nonresponse in general, and attrition in particular, is among the most important biases afflicting longitudinal studies. Though surveys often try to minimize the problem (e.g., by re-weighting the observations), this can potentially lead to significant bias in the estimates. However, in the three studies we referred to, neither attrition nor nonresponse seem to have much of an effect.

First, as far as the NLSY79 is concerned, attrition is not considered much of a problem—in fact, as Randall Olsen writes in the 2005 issue of *Monthly Labor Review*, which commemorates 25 years of NLSY79, "The National Longitudinal Survey of Youth in 1979 (NLSY79) .... is the gold standard for sample retention against which longitudinal surveys are usually measured."[79]

Second, Zahs et al. (1995) have a detailed discussion of attrition or nonresponse bias in the High School and Beyond Survey.[80] They conclude that, with a few minor qualifications, "the results consistently indicate that nonresponse had a small impact on base-year and follow-up estimates," and that this is true of both the school-level bias component and the student-level bias component.

As the above discussion on the NELS:88 shows, attrition is unlikely to have biased the results in any significant way.

A Rand study in 1999,[81] which used data from the first follow-up of HSB and the second follow-up of NELS, found that with the proper adjustments the follow-up samples could be made to look like the base-year samples.

APPENDIX B
Case studies based on longitudinal data from Florida, Chicago, and New York City

The presence of longitudinal data, which track individual students over their high school years, allows us to compute the 'true' graduation rates and compare them to these recently proposed measures. The longitudinal data are drawn from the same underlying school records as the Swanson-UI and Greene measures yet arrive at different answers for both the level of graduation and its trend.

The characteristics and quality of student longitudinal data at state and local levels are not yet fully established. We have considered where longitudinal graduation rates may be biased because of a possible faulty characterization of some groups as 'leavers.' However, we have little doubt that any corrections to the methods of New York City and Florida would still show much higher graduation rates that the Swanson-UI and Greene measures. Thus, the available state and city longitudinal data provide an additional reason for skepticism about the accuracy and utility of the Swanson-UI and Greene measures.

We first discuss graduation rates in Florida, where we have five-year graduation rates for the classes of 2002 and 2003 and four-year graduation rates for earlier classes. This is followed by comparing graduation rates in the Chicago Public Schools, where we have data on each graduating class from 1996 to 2004. We then turn to New York City, which has the longest historical series.

Graduation rates from Florida
The Florida Department of Education has been publishing cohort-based graduation rates since 1999-2000.[82] They publish both four-year and five-year graduation rates.[83] Since the latter are available only for 2001-02 and 2002-03, we calculate all the different measures of graduation rates for these two years and show them in **Table B-1**.[84]

Two points about these graduation rates should be noted at the outset. First, students who transfer into adult education programs are removed from the cohort in the same manner as students who transfer into other public school systems, private schools, or home education programs. For the 2004-05 school year, about 6% of the cohort transferred to adult education programs, and less than 1% transferred to home education. Many of the people enrolled in adult education and home education programs receive diplomas. However, students who transfer to adult education programs not administered by the district education system but by community colleges or other entities do not have their data reported to the state database used for calculating the graduation rate, and hence are excluded.

Similarly, since in Florida a GED certificate is considered on par with a regular diploma for purposes of graduation, the graduation rate calculations mentioned above include GEDs. For 2004-05, the only year we could get data

APPENDIX TABLE B-1 Florida: Comparing the four-year and five-year cohort graduation rates with recent estimates

	Swanson (CPI)	Greene	Warren (ECR)	9th grade to diploma	8th grade to diploma	Cohort graduation rate		Error compared to the 5-year cohort graduation rate				
						four-year	five-year	Swanson (CPI)	Greene	Warren (ECR)	9th grade to diploma	8th grade to diploma
Total												
Cohort graduating in 2002	56.9%	59%	63.0%	55.7%	68.7%	67.9%	72.4%	15.5	13.4	9.4	16.7	3.7
Cohort graduating in 2003	57.7	61.8	65.0	56.7	70.8	69.0	73.3	15.6	11.5	8.3	16.6	2.5
Non-Hispanic white												
Cohort graduating in 2002	62.3%	67.1%	70.3%	60.7%	70.7%	75.9%	80%	17.7	12.9	9.7	19.3	9.3
Cohort graduating in 2003	65.4	69.6	72.5	62.0	73.3	78.1	81.6	16.2	12.0	9.1	19.6	8.3
Non-Hispanic black												
Cohort graduating in 2002	45%	49.7%	54.5%	44.2%	59%	54.9%	59.7%	14.7	10.0	5.2	15.5	0.7
Cohort graduating in 2003	42.7	51.4	54.6	43.2	58.8	54.2	59.2	16.5	7.8	4.6	16.0	0.4
Hispanics												
Cohort graduating in 2002	55.1%	50%	54.2%	55.3%	72.6%	60.1%	65.1%	10.0	15.1	10.9	9.8	-7.5
Cohort graduating in 2003	53.6	53.2	56.2	56.6	73.7	61.1	66.1	12.5	12.9	9.9	9.5	-7.6

Notes: All graduation measures shown, except the cohort graduation rates, are from authors' calculations, based on data from the CCD (except diploma figures for 2002-03, which are based on the Florida Dept of Education). The cohort graduation rates are based on various Florida Department of Education publications, see Appendix B for details. The Greene (Warren) estimates adjust for changes in population between the 8th (9th) and 12th grades.

Source: U.S. Department of Education, Common Core of Data (CCD).

on, inclusion of GEDs biases the four-year cohort graduation rate upwards by 2.2 percentage points overall. Importantly, the bias is bigger for whites (3.3 percentage points) than for blacks (1.1 percentage points) and Hispanics (1.0 percentage point).

Some interesting conclusions emerge from the table. Both the four-year and the five-year cohort graduation rates are significantly higher than each of the other measures. The gaps are largest for the ninth-grade-to-diploma and the Swanson-UI measures, with more than 15 percentage point differences for all groups except Hispanics, for which the difference is still around 10 percentage points. Of the three recent measures proposed, Warren's ECR does the best, but even here the differences are in general around 10 percentage points except for non-Hispanic blacks. Generally, the simple eighth-grade-to-diploma measure is the closest to the five-year cohort-graduation rate (but still about 3.0 percentage points too low) but seems an inappropriate proxy since it significantly overstates the Hispanic graduation rate (by about 7.5 percentage points) and understates the non-Hispanic white rate (by about 9.0 percentage points).[85] While it is true that the cohort graduation rates are slightly biased upward, due to inclusion of GEDs and treating students who transfer to adult education programs, who might have lower rates of completion with a diploma, as transfers, these comparisons strongly suggest that the recently proposed measures of calculating graduation rates fall significantly short of replicating the true or underlying picture. (The NCLB rate—an on-time measure of graduation—does not include GEDs.)

Though estimates of five-year cohort graduation rates are not available prior to 2002-03, we have estimates for four-year cohort graduation rates since 1996-97, and race-specific four-year estimates since 1999-2000. These rates are shown in **Figures B-A, B-B, B-C, and B-D**. Figure B-A shows the overall cohort graduation rates since 1996-97, and compares them to estimates from other measures—Swanson-UI and Warren and Greene. Not only are the recent measures significantly lower than the cohort graduation rates, the trends are also often different.[86] Actually, the Swanson-UI and Greene rates are even lower than the NCLB rate, which is itself significantly downward biased because of non-inclusion of special diplomas and because it is a four-year rate (the diploma data used by Swanson-UI and Greene include diplomas granted later than four years, which one can see from the different cohort rates are nontrivial).

Figures B-B, B-C, and B-D show the graduation rates for whites, blacks, and Hispanics separately. In each case, the Swanson-UI measure or the Greene measures yields the lowest graduation rates—Greene also generally gets the trends wrong.

Graduation rates from Chicago

The Consortium on Chicago School Research, which conducts research on Chicago's public schools, has published graduation rates for Chicago Public Schools (CPS) since the graduating class of 1996 (Allensworth 2005). These

FIGURE B-A Graduation rates in Florida, 1997-2004

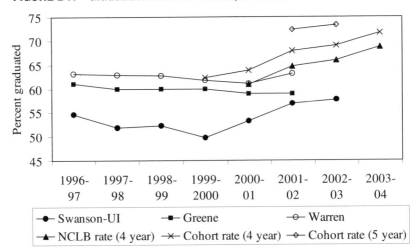

Source: The NCLB rate and the cohort rates (four-year and five-year) are from publications of the Florida Department of Education, see Appendix B for details. The Greene numbers are from Greene and Winters (2005), while the Warren numbers are from Warren (2005). The Swanson-UI numbers are based on authors' calculations using enrollment and diploma numbers from the CCD and the Florida Dept. of Education.

FIGURE B-B Graduation rates in Florida, whites, 2000-04

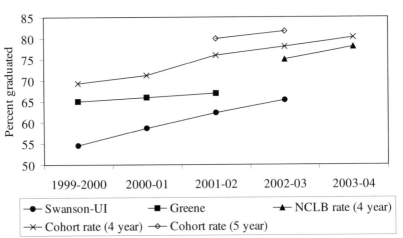

Source: The NCLB rate and the cohort rates (four-year and five-year) are from publications of the Florida Department of Education, see Appendix B for details. The Greene numbers are from Greene and Winters (2005). The Swanson-UI numbers are based on authors' calculations using enrollment and diploma numbers from the CCD and the Florida Dept. of Education.

FIGURE B-C   Graduation rates in Florida, blacks, 2000-04

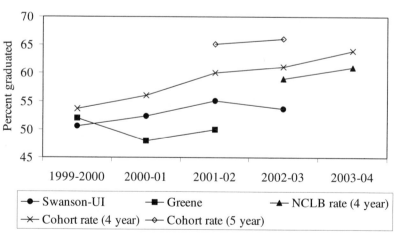

Source: The NCLB rate and the cohort rates (four-year and five-year) are from publications of the Florida Department of Education, see Appendix B for details. The Greene numbers are from Greene and Winters (2005). The Swanson-UI numbers are based on authors' calculations using enrollment and diploma numbers from the CCD and the Florida Dept. of Education.

FIGURE B-D   Graduation rates in Florida, Hispanics, 2000-04

Source: The NCLB rate and the cohort rates (four-year and five-year) are from publications of the Florida Department of Education, see Appendix B for details. The Greene numbers are from Greene and Winters (2005). The Swanson-UI numbers are based on authors' calculations using enrollment and diploma numbers from the CCD and the Florida Dept. of Education.

APPENDIX TABLE B-2   Graduation rates of beginning Chicago Public Schools ninth graders, four years later

Cohort (9th grade began in fall)	Four-year graduation rate	9th grade to diploma	CPI (9th grade)
1992	45.7%	48.2%	49%
1993	47.8	48.8	41.7
1994	47.7	50.4	42.2
1995	49.3	46.7	43.9
1996	50.9	42.4	44.9
1997	48.5	41.2	48.8
1998	50.2	45.5	50.9
1999	54.1	46.7	52.0
2000	54.3	48.9	

Note: Graduates are defined as students who received a regular high school diploma. Recipients of alternative school diplomas and GEDs are not counted as graduates. Dropouts are students who were recorded as dropouts or lost students, left school without a leave reason, or enrolled in an alternative school and did not transfer back to a regular school. "Left CPS are defined as students who are no longer active in CPS, who were recorded as leaving for any of the following reasons: transferred to a regular (non-alternative) school, institutionalized, or deceased. Graduation rate is calculated as the percent of graduates divided by (1 - percent who left CPS).

Source: The numbers for the four-year graduation rate come from Allensworth (2005), Table 1. The Swanson-UI numbers and the ninth-grade-to-diploma numbers have been calculated from the City of Chicago School District figures from CCD.

completion rates are based on individual student records and hence present an accurate picture of high school completion by entering ninth graders. **Table B-2** (and **Figure B-E**) shows the graduation rates of successive cohorts of CPS students, where graduation is defined as on-time or four-year graduation with a regular diploma. As is evident, the four-year graduation rate (based on individual records) tends to be greater than both the Swanson-UI and the ninth-grade-to-diploma measures. This is especially true when one notes that the CCD-based measures include all diplomas, including those earned in a fifth or sixth year, whereas the longitudinal data reports only diplomas earned by the fourth year. So the differences will be even more pronounced if we compare the CCD-based measures to the five-year or six-year completion rate, as we should for a correct comparison.[87]

Perhaps more important, the trends are often quite different between the accurate longitudinal data and the latter two CCD-based measures. For instance, the longitudinal data show a steadily climbing graduation rate whereas the CCD rates can show a corresponding deterioration (consider the Swanson-UI up until 1996 or the diploma/ninth-grade ratio up to 1998 and 1999).

These comparisons of Chicago data suggest that the newly conventional CCD-based measures of high school graduation incorrectly estimate the extent of graduation as well as the trend in graduation rates.

FIGURE B-E   **Graduation rates in Chicago public schools, 1996-2003**

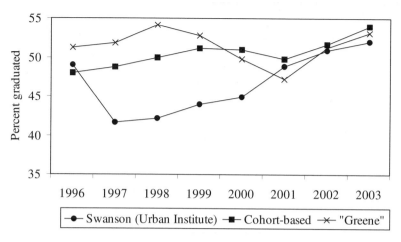

Notes: For the cohort-based measure, we assume that 13 year olds correspond to 8th grade - i.e., 13-year olds in 1991-92 correspond to eighth graders in 1991-92 and henceto the graduating class of 1996.

Source: The CPI and Greene measures are based on calculations using enrollment and diploma data on City of Chicago School District from the CCD database. Diploma data for 2002-03 and 2003-04 are from the Illinois State Board of Education, http://www.isbe.net/research/htmls/eoy_report.htm. The Greene measure is unadjusted for changes in population during high school years.

Table B-3 presents longitudinally measured graduation rates for each race/ethnic gender category for Chicago public schools starting with the cohort of 13-year-olds in 1991. Graduation rates at age 18 and at age 19 are both shown. Girls are more likely to graduate than boys within each ethnic/race group, with the greatest gap among blacks. Graduation rates rose over this time period among each race/ethnic/gender category. For instance, the rate at which young black men graduate has inched up from about 35% for the entering cohort in 1991, but remained abysmally low—less than 40%—for the most recent cohort. Young white men have graduation rates approaching 60% at age 19, which is well short of the national average (about 75% for the CCD-based measures and ten percentage points more in other studies). This table amply reminds us that regardless of the method of measurement, high school graduation in Chicago (as perhaps in other cities) is disappointingly, and unacceptably, low.

Graduation rates from New York City

We have also examined longitudinal data on high school completion with diplomas (excluding GEDs) from New York City public schools, which tracks cohorts of entering ninth graders till their graduation or dropping out four, five

APPENDIX TABLE B-3   Graduation rates in Chicago, by race and gender

	Males				Females			
	White	Black	Hispanic	Asian	White	Black	Hispanic	Asian
Graduated by age 18								
13-year olds in fall of:								
1991	35.9%	26.8%	30.5%	52.9%	49.5%	44.5%	43.9%	59.9%
1992	37.5	26.3	33.4	54.2	49.7	47.4	45.7	72.9
1993	39.0	28.2	34.1	57.8	52.9	48.0	47.9	69.5
1994	41.7	29.6	37.9	60.8	54.3	48.3	51.5	69.4
1995	41.5	30.3	38.4	58.6	53.2	48.6	50.9	72.0
1996	41.1	27.9	32.7	55.8	54.0	45.8	47.8	72.7
1997	41.1	28.3	33.8	59.6	53.1	46.2	50.3	68.0
1998	44.4	29.0	37.9	58.9	56.7	48.2	52.5	72.0
1999	46.2	30.8	39.6	59.2	60.2	49.0	53.7	74.7
Graduated by age 19								
13-year olds in fall of:								
1991	48.9%	35.0%	44.1%	72.6%	63.0%	52.6%	55.8%	79.2%
1992	50.7	34.3	44.1	72.6	63.3	54.5	56.9	87.1
1993	52.4	35.5	47.0	75.0	66.1	55.2	58.6	83.9
1994	55.1	36.8	48.5	76.5	66.7	54.4	61.7	82.1
1995	54.2	37.3	48.3	72.5	64.8	54.4	60.5	86.0
1996	55.0	35.8	44.2	71.3	67.9	53.4	59.5	84.5
1997	55.2	37.5	47.8	76.3	69.5	53.6	63.0	84.0
1998	57.5	38.5	51.2	76.2	71.2	57.1	64.8	84.8

Graduation and dropout rates include in the denominator students still enrolled in school.

Source: Allensworth 2005, Table 3.1.

and up to seven years later. These numbers are shown in **Table B-4** and **Figure B-F**, beginning with the class of 1996. For purposes of comparison, we also show the corresponding Swanson-UI and basic completion ratios, computed from the CCD enrollment and diploma data. This comparison gives us an additional chance to compare the 'true graduation rate' using student longitudinal data against various proxies of the graduation rate compiled from the enrollment and diploma data generated by the same underlying data.[88]

The rate of high school completion with a regular diploma (excluding GEDs),[89] three years after expected graduation, was about 58.2% for the class of 1996, rising slightly to 60.4% for the class of 2001. However, both the Swanson-UI and the ninth-grade-to-diploma measures yield significantly lower completion rates—the corresponding figures are 36.3% and 39.3% (Swanson-UI), and 41.4% and 36.6% (ninth-grade-to-diploma). There is a 20 percentage point gap between the Swanson-UI and the 'true graduation rate,' a remarkable inaccuracy. Even taking the average of eighth, ninth, and tenth grades—a rough proxy for the Greene measure (without the migration adjustment)—

APPENDIX TABLE B-4 Graduation rates from New York City

Graduating class	Longitudinal (NYC Dept. of Ed.) (diplomas only, excluding GEDs & certificates.) (3 yrs after exp. grad.)	Swanson-UI	9th grade to diploma	8th grade to diploma	Average of 8th, 9th & 10th grades to diploma
1987		43.8%			
1988		40.6			
1989		35.7			
1990		43.5	41.5%		
1991		39.3	39.6	57.4%	45.9%
1992		43.9	44.2	62.5	50.9
1993		40.2	42.2	60.3	49.0
1994		38.2	41.9	61.3	48.7
1995		37.8	39.4	56.8	45.8
1996	58.2%	36.3	41.4	61.0	48.4
1997	59.0	33.8	39.8	59.8	47.4
1998	58.7	31.2	39.6	58.4	46.8
1999		35.0	38.9	59.8	47.4
2000	60.2	37.7	36.8	58.1	44.7
2001	60.4	39.3	36.6	58.4	45.5
2002		36.8	35.2	56.3	44.0

Notes: The graduation rates under Longitudinal have been compiled from Table 3 (total number of graduates) and Table 2 (breakdown of graduation type). The other graduation rates have been calculated using the CCD enrollment and diploma for the New York City Public Schools.

Source: New York City Department of Education, Final Longitudinal Report, class of 2001.

significantly understates completion, and gets the trend wrong.[90] These inaccuracies should not be surprising when one realizes that there is a ninth grade bulge (the degree to which ninth-grade enrollment exceeds eighth-grade enrollment, thus being a poor proxy for 'entering ninth graders') in New York City of from 40% to 60% over the last 17 years. The eighth-grade-to-diploma measure comes closest to replicating the cohort-based graduation rate in levels, though even here the trends look different—the true rate is rising while the proxy is falling.

FIGURE B-F   Graduation rates in New York City, 1996-2002

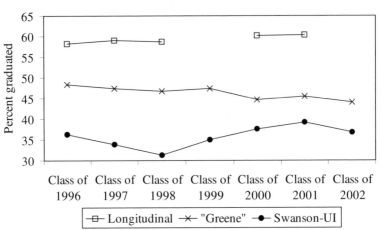

Source: The Swanson-UI and Greene measures are based on calculations using enrollment and diploma data on New York City Public Schools from the CCD database.
The Greene measure is unadjusted for changes in population during high school years.
The source for the longitudinal rate is various reports of the New York City Department of Education (http://www.nycenet.edu/daa/reports), in particular The Class of 2001 Final Longitudinal Report.

APPENDIX C
Methodology of the Integrated Public Use Microdata Series (IPUMS) data analysis

The following is a brief description of the main steps involved in calculating graduation rates from the 2000 census microdata (IPUMS).

The IPUMS data of the 2000 census classify people into two groups— those living in "group quarters" and those not living in "group quarters." Those living in group quarters are further classified into four groups:[91]

i)   Institutions
ii) Non-institutional group quarters
iii) Military
iv) College dormitory

We define civilian non-institutional population to include those not living in group quarters, plus those in non-institutions and college dorms. Thus, we end up with three mutually exclusive and exhaustive categories—civilian non-institutional, institutional, and military.

Similarly, we divide people into different racial groups based on responses to questions about Hispanic origin (hispan) and race (race).[92] First, we code everyone who responded "yes" to a question about Hispanic origin as Hispanic. Of those responding "no" to this question, we assign race according to their responses to questions about race (race). Note that people who said that they were of Hispanic origin and also mentioned white as their race subsequently are coded as Hispanics. The final racial categories are non-Hispanic whites, non-Hispanic blacks, Hispanics, Asians and Pacific Islanders, American Indians, and "Others"—the last is a hybrid category which includes those non-Hispanics whose racial status could not be ascertained.[93]

Similarly, we classify people into different educational categories based on responses to questions about educational attainment (educ99). This variable indicates the respondent's highest level of educational attainment. Respondents without high school diplomas were to indicate the highest school grade they had completed, while those with high school diplomas were to indicate the highest diploma or degree they had obtained. Educ99 was disaggregated into 18 categories in the original data—since we are mostly interested in high school completion we aggregated this into the following six categories:

1) No school completed
2) Nursery or kindergarten completed
3) First through fourth grades completed
4) Fifth through eighth grades completed
5) Ninth through twelfth grades, no diploma[94]
6) High school graduate or GED and beyond

Next we define recent immigrants to be foreign-born people living in the United States for less than 15 years. This status is calculated from the variable yrsusa1, which was asked of all foreign-born persons and persons born in U.S. outlying areas and indicates how long each foreign-born person had been living in the United States.[95] For the nation as a whole, slightly over 14% in the age group 25-29 in 2000 are recent immigrants, the rest (about 86%) have been in the United States for more than 15 years.[96]

Two final points are in order. First, we focus on the age-group 25-29, since most other studies in the literature do so. Second, sometimes we use the Census Bureau weights instead of the IPUMS weights for the different categories—civilian non-institutional, institutional, and military. The Census Bureau counts of military personnel includes, e.g., U.S. military reserves stationed overseas and is slightly higher than the IPUMS counts, as the following figures show. However, the results are qualitatively similar, though high school completion rates are slightly lower, if we use IPUMS weights for the three categories.

National monthly population estimates for 25-29 year olds, April 1, 2000 (Census Bureau)[97]

Resident plus Armed Forces	19,431,207	
Armed Forces overseas	49,871	(0.26%)
Armed Forces resident	238,074	(1.23%)
Institutional	348,932	(1.80%)
Civilian Non-Institutional	18,794,330	(96.72%)

In IPUMS 2000, for both 1% and 5% microdata samples, the percentage of people in institutions is 1.69%, close to the Census Bureau number above, but that in the military is only 0.25%.

Endnotes

1. These studies are referenced and discussed in detail in sections I and III. Important contributions include Greene and Forster (2003), Greene and Winters (2005), Miao and Haney (2004), Swanson (2003, 2004), and Warren (2005).

2. Phillip Kaufman, in a paper presented at the Harvard University Civil Rights Project Conference on Dropout Research in 2001 (Kaufman 2001) said:

> What can we learn from these comparisons? One conclusion is that the various datasets give approximately similar answers when asked similar questions. That is, differences in published dropout rates from these data sources are due more to differences in definitions and target populations than to differences in their methods....The exception to this general rule of correspondence among data sources is the dropout data generated by the CCD....While it may be that the CPS data are overestimates and the CCD data are closer to reality, the fact that other CPS estimates appear to be consistent with NELS estimates argue in favor of the CPS estimates. (p. 18-20, 27)

3. Table 23-1, *The Condition of Education 2005* (NCES 2005–094), U.S. Department of Education, National Center for Education Statistics, Washington, DC: U.S. Government Printing Office, available online at http://nces.ed.gov/programs/coe/2005/section3/table.asp?tableID=428. The report does not break down completions into regular diplomas and alternative credentials like GEDs.

4. See http://www.census.gov/population/www/socdemo/educ-attn.html.

5. Often, enrollment data from the CCD are augmented by estimates of demographic change from the Census Bureau. See Section III for details.

6. See http://www.ed.gov/about/offices/list/ovae/pi/hsinit/papers/nclb.pdf, page 1.

7. The NELS:88, which is the most relevant study for our purposes, starts with students in the spring of their eighth grade year.

8. The measures of graduation rates proposed in recent studies either look at successive cohorts (Swanson-Urban Institute) or adjust for entry and exit of students from a particular cohort by estimates drawn from the Census Bureau (Greene and Winters (2005), Greene and Forster (2003), Warren (2005)). As we discuss later in Sections III and VIII, both of these yield estimates that are significantly different from these longitudinal studies.

9. See http://nces.ed.gov/pubsearch/getpubcats.asp?sid=023.

10. This discussion is based on different NCES publications relating to the NELS:88 survey (http://nces.ed.gov/pubsearch/getpubcats.asp?sid=023), particularly Ingels et al. (1995).

11. The process referred to as 'freshening' added students who were not in the base-year sampling frame, either because they were not in the country or because they were not in eighth grade in the spring term of 1988. The 1990 (1992) freshening process

provided a representative sample of students enrolled in tenth (twelfth) grade in the spring of 1990 (1992).

12. Schools selected for the contextual components of the second follow-up — the school administrator and teacher surveys — are referred to as contextual schools. Sample members enrolled in those schools are referred to as contextual students.

13. Triple ineligibles are sample members who were ineligible for the base year, first follow-up, and second follow-up surveys due to mental or physical disability, or language barrier.

14. This sampling design allowed for maximizing the number of students kept in the study (and for whom transcripts were collected) while keeping costs down by minimizing the number of schools interviewers needed to travel to for administration of the survey. The high transcript response rate along with the fact that the data were collected from a large number of the original sample members implies that any potential bias was kept to a minimum.

15. These data are taken from Adelman (2006), Table L1. Note that, as the description says, " In addition to regular interviews with these students, the data set on which this essay draws includes the critical components of high school and college transcripts, and the transcript data are the principal sources for the academic history observed" - so the bias from self-reporting is minimal.

16. See the article by BLS economist Julie Yates (2005) for more information on the NLSY. Appendix A also provides some information on the methodology of the NLSY.

17. See http://nces.ed.gov/pubsearch/getpubcats.asp?sid=022.

18. Because of changes in definition and sampling framework, it is not possible to simply compare graduation rates across these different longitudinal surveys, without first making necessary adjustments. See Kaufman (1996) for more on this.

19. For a list of Swanson's work in this field, please see http://www.urban.org/expert.cfm?ID=ChristopherBSwanson.

20. The data on eighth and ninth grade enrollments are taken from the CCD Web site.

21. Some researchers have argued that since students transfer (net) from private schools to public schools between the eighth and ninth grades, using eighth grade as the base may underestimate the size of the entering ninth grade public school cohort. Using enrollment in private and public schools as estimated by the Census Bureau (http://www.census.gov/population/www/socdemo/school/cps2004.html) we find that the increase in ninth grade enrollment in public schools (relative to eighth grade) from this source is likely to be small —3% overall but only 2% for blacks and 1% for Hispanics. This is discussed further in this section.

22. See Miao and Haney (2004) for further information on this.

23. Since disaggregated data on enrollment by race are not available for all of the states, we use only the 40 states that have data for all the years (1992-93 to 2003-04). These states account for 83% of white enrollment, 83% of black enrollment, and 90% of Hispanic enrollment, so the bias from omission of the remaining 11 states is likely to be minimal. (These percentages are for 2002-03, when all states have data on enrollment by race.) Note that the numbers for *Total* in Figure A include all the 50 states.

24. Data from Texas for the years 2002-03 and 2003-04 show that about 17% of all ninth graders are repeaters (see: http://www.tea.state.tx.us/research/pdfs/retention_2003-04.pdf, page 16).

25. Retention rates seem to decline from grade to grade, thereby distorting the year-by-year attrition computed in the Swanson-UI measure.

26. We compute the impact of transfers from eighth grade to ninth grade based on the change in the shares of enrollment in private schools between elementary and secondary schools for each race/ethnic group (http://www.census.gov/population/www/socdemo/school/cps2004.html).

27. In earlier papers, Greene had used eighth grade enrollment in year x, adjusted for changes in the total student population between years x and x+4, as the denominator, while using the number of diplomas issued in year x+4 as the numerator. Later papers use an average of eighth, ninth and tenth grade enrollments instead of eighth grade enrollment alone, and adjusts this by the difference in the number of 14-year olds in year x from the number of 17-year olds in year x+3. We found that a simple averaging of eighth, ninth, and tenth grade enrollments, while attenuating the bias from the ninth-grade 'bulge', does not adequately solve the problem.

28. Warren does not compute the ECR for specific ethnic groups, such as whites or Hispanics.

29. See http://www.urban.org/url.cfm?ID=900794.

30. See http://www.ed-data.k12.ca.us/Navigation/fsTwoPanel.asp?bottom=%2Fprofile%2Easp%3Flevel%3D04%26reportNumber%3D16.

31. All these figures are from the graduating class of 2002.

32. See http://www.census.gov/population/www/socdemo/education.html#attainment.

33. The Department of Education also publishes statistics on public school dropouts and completers, drawn from the Common Core of Data (CCD) survey system of the National Center for Education Statistics (NCES). See for example Young (2003). These statistics have also come under intense scrutiny; in addition to the references already listed, see Barton (2004).

34. We have not been able to identify any studies which present any evidence on self-reporting bias and the issue is hardly mentioned, except for those invoking it in the measurement of high school completion.

35. The overall graduation rate in the 2000 census for people aged 25-29 was 83.8%, rising to 87.8% if we exclude the recent immigrants (those who immigrated to the US during or after their high school years). The overall graduation rate in the March 2000 CPS for people aged 25-29 was 88.1% (civilian non-institutionalized population). (The graduation rate in the 2000 census for civilian non-institutionalized population is 84.1%—so this is about 4 percentage points less than the CPS.) In the NELS data (Table 1) the graduation rate at around age 26 is 90.7%. (All these figures include GEDs, since unlike the NELS the census and the CPS do not differentiate between a GED and a regular diploma.)

36. See http://www.bls.census.gov/cps/basic/perfmeas/coverage.htm.

37. A coverage ratio compares the estimate from the sample of the number of people who have a particular characteristic to the same estimate from updated decennial census figures. For example, a coverage ratio of .95 for males aged 50 to 59 indicates that the CPS estimate of the number of persons in this subpopulation is 95% of the updated census population estimate.

38. "In the CPS, coverage ratios are examined for various age/race/sex groupings. Prior to publication, adjustments are made to the household weights using population control totals from the updated census estimates. This ensures the estimated population from CPS is comparable to the updated census estimates for these particular groupings" (from the Web page on coverage ratios, CPS, Bureau of Labor Statistics, http:// www.bls.census.gov/cps/basic/perfmeas/coverage.htm).

39. As an analogy, consider a school cafeteria where some students eat salads while the others go for burgers. If burgers were to be banned beginning tomorrow, say, then some of the students currently eating burgers would presumably switch to salads, instead of going hungry. The important point is that, though the GEDs might have been originally intended as a 'second chance' for students who could not complete high school for different reasons, many current high school students opt for GEDs quite early, as attested by the increasing proportion of GED certificates (about 45% in 2000) going to people aged 19 years or less.

40. Microdata from the 2000 census show that for the United States as a whole the percentage of people in the age group 25-29 residing in institutions is 1.69%, while the percentage that has been in the United States for less than 15 years is about 14%. For black men, however, the percentage living in institutions is 12.4%.

41. For more information on IPUMS, and how to access these publicly available data, see http://www.ipums.org.

42. For a full list of variables that are available, see http://www.ipums.org/usa/ vars.html, where variables are divided into household record and person record.

43. This bias due to inclusion of recent immigrants has been known for a while, but not always adequately emphasized. For example, in Kaufman et al, (2004) the graduation rate for Hispanics born outside the U.S. is only about 50.3%, while those of first generation Hispanics and second generation Hispanics are 78.2% and 81.5%, respectively (Table 4, p. 21). See also an earlier report by Marilyn McMillen (1995), *Dropout Rates in The United States: 1995*, Tables 15 and 16 (http://nces.ed.gov/pubs97/ 97473.pdf).

44. Since the IPUMS does not differentiate between a regular diploma and a GED, the results in this section relate to overall high school completion. In section VIII we combine these results with estimates of the share of each race/ethnic group with a GED to obtain estimates of high school completion based on a regular diploma.

45. We have experimented with some alternate numbers—the results are not sensitive to the particular cutoff used and are available from the authors on request.

46. The educational attainment of the black institutional population lags behind that of the white institutional population, but is greater than that of the Hispanic institutional population.

47. These are work disability, disability limiting mobility, personal care limitation, physical difficulty, difficulty remembering, and vision or hearing difficulty (see http://www.ipums.org/usa/person.html#pdisability). The majority of people with these limitations have completed high school, but their graduation rate is significantly below that of the general (non-disabled) population. (Of course, we do not know when the disability was contracted — it may be after high school years.)

48. These data are published by the Census Bureau using the March CPS series.

49. This is based on our computations of the decennial census data for 2000.

50. Using just the beginning and end years, 1994 and 2004, would show a sizable improvement in completion rates among black men. Data for the 1990 to 1993 period suggest that 1994 is not an outlier, so one could say there was substantial improvement for black men since the early 1990s.

51. Shares of black men in prison presented in Figure G for the 1999-2004 period are based on inmates in state and federal prisons and those in local jails from: http://www.ojp.usdoj.gov/bjs/pub/pdf/pjim99.pdf and other issues of *Prison and Jail Inmates at Midyear*. The 1994-99 data are extrapolated from the growth of the total black male prison and jail population: (http://www.ojp.usdoj.gov/bjs/pub/pdf/p96.pdf), Table 11 and later annual reports; and, http://www.ojp.usdoj.gov/bjs/glance/tables/jailracetab.htm. Total black male population computed from the CPS with the addition of the correctional population.

52. We compute the civilian completion rate as the weighted average of the civilian non-institutional population and the correctional and the non-institutional civilian populations. The prior footnote provides the sources for the population estimates. The CPS provides the completion rate for the non-institutional civilian populations and the Census provided the completion rate—52%—for the institutional population (somewhat broader than corrections).

53. Data provided by Yates from the NLSY show that of those blacks who left their initial schooling with a GED, 56.5% returned to school and 35% had some college education, though none received a college degree. Rumberger and Lamb (2003), however, find that the rate of attending postsecondary institutions was significantly lower among former dropouts who completed (mostly with a GED) compared to high school graduates who never dropped out.

54. Thomas Kane and Cecilia Rouse (1995a) show that even those who enter but fail to complete degrees at community colleges earn significantly more than high school dropouts. In another study they find that the average person who attended a two-year college earned about 10% more than those without any college education, even without completing an associate's degree (1995b).

55. John Tyler, Richard Murnane, and J. Willett (2000) show that the GED signal increases the earnings of young white dropouts by 10 to 19%. In a more recent paper using a unique data set constructed from Florida GED and unemployment insurance (UI) administrative records to estimate the impact of the GED on the earnings of high school dropouts who seek the credential, Tyler (2004) finds that the acquisition of a GED leads to greater quarterly earnings growth.

56. These data are based on the number of GED credentials issued by age provided by the American Council on Education for Table 105 in the Digest of Education Statistics, 2003 (data up to 2001) and an update provided to us with data through 2003. The data are presented by the age when the GED was earned. We accumulated these measures to derive the number of GEDs for those ages 25-29. This involved some simple assumptions such as there being an equal number of GEDs granted for each age within the 20-24-year-old group in any particular year. We divided the total GEDs in the 25-29 year group by the population.

57. Correspondence with an analyst at the Census Bureau indicates that they do not have faith in their measurement of GEDs in the CPS. Nor does NCES have faith in their counts of GEDs in the CCD: NCES now reports ACE data on GEDs rather than reports from the states.

58. The Census and CPS data are all for 2000. NELS is eight years after the normal completion time of the class of 1992 which corresponds to roughly age 26.

59. The bias in 2000 from an incarceration rate of 13.9% in 2000 is to artificially raise completion for black men by 4.9%. Consequently, we lower the overall black completion rate by 2.5 percentage points (because there was no bias for black women).

60. We do not have the GED breakdown for the NLSY97 data and therefore use the NLSY79 data.

61. We could not find published numbers for the Swanson-UI index for any graduating class prior to 2001. In the bottom half of Table 10, we calculate the Swanson-UI index for the class of 1994—the earliest class for which enrollment data by grade and race are available for most states. Note that the published numbers for Swanson-UI index are based on aggregation of school-level data, while we use state-level data in our replications. However, the bias from this is minimal, as the school-level and state-level measures yield almost identical estimates.

62. These ratios of diplomas in year x over eighth (ninth) grade enrollment in year x-4 (x-3) are often called the Basic Completion Rates, see Warren (2005). Also, as mentioned earlier, the class of 1994 is the first class on which we have enrollment and diploma data disaggregated by grade and race (1992-93 is the first year with enrollment data disaggregated by grade and race).

63. If there is a significant amount of in-transfer of students after the ninth grade—net immigration for the United States as a whole—and if these students enroll in U.S. high schools and obtain diplomas, then the basic completion rates will overstate high school completion. However, even though this might be a significant factor for individual states or school districts, for the United States as a whole this is unlikely to be a major factor. As we saw in the IPUMS data, recent immigrants have much lower levels of educational attainment and it is unlikely most of them ever attended a high school in the United States, even though they may be physically present in the country during part of their high school years. Again, this underscores the superiority of looking at graduation rates from longitudinal studies which track individual students over time.

64. Greene also adjusts for population growth over the period but this adjustment has little effect nationally.

65. Note, however, that as we found in the IPUMS, not many of these in-migrants will complete high school in the United States—unlikely that many of them will even attend one. So the extent of bias may not be large. However, given that Warren's migration adjustment for this cohort is about 5.6%—implying that the size of this cohort increased by 5.6% between the eighth and twelfth grades—this may still bias the calculated graduation rate upwards by 2-3 percentage points.

66. The exact formula for the ECR is

$$ECR = \frac{\text{High School Completers}_{\text{Spring of Academic Year x}}}{\text{Estimated \# of First - time 9th graders}_{\text{Fall of Academic Year x-3}} * \textit{Migration Adjustment}}$$

67. If we do not restrict ourselves to on-time completion we find that 83% of 1988 eighth graders in the NELS had completed high school with a regular diploma by spring 1994 (http://nces.ed.gov/pubs2005/2005026.pdf, Table 1, page 1). This is considerably higher than Warren's comparable figure of 78.4%, which itself is possibly slightly overestimated due to inclusion of diplomas obtained by immigrants who came to the country after age 13 (or eighth grade). (The NELS figure includes both public and private school students, but because private schools enroll less than 10% of all high school students the bias on that account is likely to be minimal, less than 1%.) Note also that as Warren points out (page 18), the ECR comes closest to the NELS figure—the CPI, for example, equals only 71.2% in 1992, a difference of about 13 percentage points.

68. Minorities are much less likely to be in private schools than whites—recent data from the October 2004 CPS show that while 14% of whites attend private schools at the elementary level, the figures for blacks and Hispanics are both about 5%. The respective figures at the high school level are 10% for whites, 3% for blacks and 4% for Hispanics (http://www.census.gov/population/www/socdemo/school/cps2004.html).

69. Kaufman et al. (2000) has some discussion about the accuracy and comparability of estimates from the CCD and the CPS, see Appendix C. See also Kaufman's chapter in Orfield (2004) for more information about the CCD.

70. The HS&B and NELS:88 surveys are part of the National Education Longitudinal Studies (NELS) program of the National Center for Education Statistics (NCES) and were established "to study the educational, vocational, and personal development of young people beginning with their elementary or high school years, and following them over time as they begin to take on adult roles and responsibilities" (http://nces.ed.gov/surveys/hsb/). There is also an earlier longitudinal study, the National Longitudinal Study of the High School Class of 1972 (NLS-72), which followed the 1972 cohort of high school seniors through 1986. Because this survey only sampled seniors in high school, it is not very informative about dropout behavior over the high school years and we do not use it in what follows.

71. Attrition refers to the phenomenon whereby respondents from the initial base-year survey are missing from the follow-up surveys. This will lead to bias if these missing persons would have had different outcomes than their counterparts in the sample who are observed at all times.

72. This quote is taken from the brief summary on NLSY79 which appears on the NLSY79 homepage at U.S. Department of Labor's Bureau of Labor Statistics. See http://www.bls.gov/nls/y79summary.htm.

73. In 1980-83, the NLSY79 collected detailed transcript information for potential high school graduates that included coursework, grades, and attendance records.

74. This section closely follows Kaufman et al. (1999), pp. 78-80. This report, available on the Web at http://nces.ed.gov/pubs2000/2000022.pdf, has details on the NELS:88 survey framework and subsequent attrition and nonresponse rates.

75. Some particular types of schools were excluded— Bureau of Indian Affairs schools, special education schools for the handicapped, area vocational schools—that do not enroll students directly, and schools for dependents of U.S. personnel overseas. However, a recent study by the Department of Education argues that "such school-level exclusions have a very small impact on national estimates" (Kaufman et al. 1999, 78).

76. Note that a case could be made for calculating the graduation rates of people with physical or mental disabilities separately from the general population, particularly if the focus is on on-time graduation with a regular diploma. These people might fail to get a regular diploma within four years, but through no fault of their own or of their schools. (Our calculations from the 2000 census microdata show that when we leave out people who report any of six forms of disabilities asked in the questionnaire, the national graduation rate increases by about 2 percentage points.)

77. The overall unweighted response rate was 94%.

78. See Kaufman et al. (1999, 79) for definition of a dropout that was used in the NELS:88.

79. http://www.bls.gov/opub/mlr/2005/02/art9full.pdf

80. See Zahs et al. (1995, 38), available online at http://nces.ed.gov/pubs95/95426.pdf. This report has a detailed analysis of nonresponse both for the base year estimates and for the subsequent first, second, third and fourth follow-ups.

81. See Koretz and Berends (2001, Chapter 3 on Data and Methods and Appendix B on Subsample Noncomparability).

82. The way these graduation rates are calculated is described in the following Florida Department of Education report (http://www.firn.edu/doe/databaseworkshop/pdf/gdcohort.pdf, page 2): "Florida's high school graduation rate is the percentage of students who graduated within four years of their initial enrollment in ninth grade. Incoming transfer students are included in the appropriate cohort based on their grade level and year of entry. Deceased students and students who withdraw to attend school in another school system are removed from the cohort. Each student in the resulting adjusted cohort receives a final classification as a graduate, dropout, or non-graduate. ("Non-graduates" include certificate recipients and retained students who remained enrolled.) Adjusted cohort = graduates + non-graduates + dropouts. Grad rate = graduates from the adjusted cohort ÷adjusted cohort."

83. See http://www.firn.edu/doe/eias/eiaspubs/pdf/gradrate.pdf.

84. We use enrollment and diploma data from the CCD (and diploma data for 2002-03 from the Florida Dept of Education) to calculate the following measures of graduation—Swanson-UI, Warren (ECR), Greene, ninth-grade-to-diploma and eighth-grade-to-diploma. For the Warren and Greene measures, which use changes in population to adjust cohort sizes, we also use data from the Census Bureau. Details are available from the authors on request.

85. One plausible reason behind this divergence for the Hispanics may be the influx of students who join after their eighth grade year, but subsequently drop out at a higher rate than those who have been continuing throughout.

86. As mentioned above, inclusion of GEDs and exclusion of transfers to adult education programs may somewhat bias upwards the cohort graduation rates. However, it is unlikely to explain the big difference between these rates.

87. "Of the students in the 1999 cohort still active after four years, 42% graduated in the following year, so that the 1999 cohort has a five-year graduation rate of 58.5%. Of the students in the 1998 cohort still active after four years, 54.5% graduated within the next two years, giving the 1998 cohort a six-year graduation rate of 56.8%" (Allensworth 2005, endnote 9).

88. There are a couple of points to note about these graduation rates. First, these measures exclude District 75, the citywide special education district which consists of schools that primarily serve students with severe disabling conditions. Second, students who entered a non-Board of Education GED preparation program are counted as transfers and not as GEDs or dropouts. While we cannot quantify the extent of bias from the second one, it is likely to be small. The first is unlikely to bias graduation rates vis-à-vis Swanson and Greene, as special education classes are ungraded and do not show up in grade-specific enrollments.

89. The New York City Public Schools breaks down completions into five categories: Local High-School Diploma, Regents-Endorsed Diploma, Regents-Endorsed Diploma with Honors, Special Education Diploma or Certificate, and GEDs. The graduation rate shown in the table includes only the first three categories.

90. We could find one published Greene estimate for New York City for the class of 1998—graduation rates of 55% (overall), 42% (blacks), 45% (Hispanics), and 80% (whites). However, we have not been able to replicate this estimate. See Greene (2002).

91. The technical name of the variable is gqtype (and gqtyped), which describes in detail the type of group quarters in which a group-quarters member resided. In the 5% sample, there are 885,357 individuals or observations who report living in non-group quarters, 15,400 observations who report living in institutions, 3,760 observations in non-institutions, 2,296 in military, and 2,283 in college dormitories.

92. The respective names of these two variables in the data set are hispan and race.

93. Many in this category report belonging to two or more categories (e.g., black and white, white and Asian, etc.). However, the percentage of the sample thus assigned is very small and unlikely to bias the results in any way.

94. This category includes those who said that they have completed twelfth grade, but without a diploma. See the detailed descriptions at http://www.ipums.org/usa/peducation/educ99a.html and http://www.ipums.org/usa/peducation/educ99b.html.

95. See http://www.ipums.org/usa/pethnicity/yrsusa1a.html.

96. We used the cutoff of 15 years since we are looking at the age-group 25-29 years, like in earlier studies, for measuring educational attainment. Most of the people in this group—25-29 years old who had been in the United States for less than 15 years—had their middle and high school education in their country of origin or birth, and their subsequent educational experience does not adequately reflect the performance or effectiveness of U.S. high schools.

97. Source: http://www.census.gov/popest/national/asrh/2003_nat_res.html.

References

Adelman, C. 2006. *The Toolbox Revisited: Paths to Degree Completion From High School Through College.* Washington, D.C.: U.S. Department of Education. http://www.ed.gov/rschstat/research/pubs/toolboxrevisit/index.html.

Allensworth, Elaine. 2005. *Graduation and Dropout Trends in Chicago: A Look at Cohorts of Students From 1991 Through 2004.* Chicago: Consortium on Chicago School Research at the University of Chicago. http://www.consortium-chicago.org/publications/p75.html.

Barton, Paul. 2004. *Unfinished Business*: *More Measured Approaches in Standards-Based Reform.* ETS Policy Information Report, available online at http://www.ets.org/Media/Education_Topics/pdf/unfinbusiness.pdf

Chaplin, Duncan. 2002. Tassels on the cheap. *Education Next.* http://www.educationnext.org/20023/24.html.

Greene, Jay P. 2002. *High School Graduation Rates in the United States.* New York, N.Y.: Manhattan Institute and Black Alliance for Educational Options. http://www.manhattan-institute.org/pdf/cr_baeo.pdf.

Greene, Jay P. and Greg Forster. 2003. *Public High School Graduation and College Readiness Rates in the United States.* Manhattan Institute. Education Working Paper 3. http://www.manhattan-institute.org/pdf/ewp_03.pdf.

Greene, Jay P. and Marcus Winters. 2005. *Public High School Graduation and College-Readiness Rates: 1991-2002.* New York, N.Y.: Manhattan Institute for Policy Research. http://www.manhattan-institute.org/html/ewp_08.htm.

Haney, Walt, George Madaus, Lisa Abrams, Anne Wheelock, Jing Miao, and Ilena Gruia. 2004. *The Education Pipeline in the United States, 1970-2000.* National Board on Educational Testing and Public Policy, Lynch School of Education, Boston College, http://www.bc.edu/research/nbetpp/statements/nbr3.pdf.

Hill, Carolyn J. and Harry Holzer. 2006. Labor Market Experiences and Transitions to Adulthood, Conference on the Economics of the Transition to Adulthood.

Ingels, Steve, Kathryn L. Dowd, John R. Taylor, Virginia H. Bartot, Martin R. Frankel, Paul A. Pulliam, and Peggy Quinn. 1995. *Second Follow-Up: Transcript Component Data File User's Manual, National Education Longitudinal Study of 1988.* Washington, D.C.: National Center for Education Statistics. March. http://nces.ed.gov/pubs95/95377.pdf.

Kane, Thomas and Cecilia Rouse. 1995a. Comment on W. Norton Grubb: The varied economic returns to postsecondary education: New evidence from the class of 1972. *The Journal of Human Resources.* Vol. 30, No. 1, pp. 205-21.

Kane, Thomas and Cecilia Rouse. 1995b. Labor market returns to two- and four-year college. *American Economic Review*, Vol. 85, No. 3, pp. 600-14.

Kaufman, Phillip. 2001. *The National Dropout Data Collection System: Assessing Consistency.* Cambridge, Mass.: The Civil Rights Project, Harvard University, http://www.civilrightsproject.harvard.edu/research/dropouts/kaufman.pdf.

Kaufman, Phillip, Jin Y. Kwon, Steve Klein, and Christopher D. Chapman. 1999. *Dropout Rates in the United States: 1998.* Washington, D.C.: U.S. Department of Education, Office of Educational Research and Improvement. NCES 2000–022.

Kaufman, Phillip, Jin Y. Kwon, Steve Klein, and Christopher D. Chapman. 2000. *Dropout Rates in the United States: 1999.* Washington, D.C.: U.S. Department of Education, National Center for Education Statistics. NCES 2001-022. http://nces.ed.gov/pubs2001/2001022.pdf.

Kaufman, P., M. N. Alt, and C. Chapman. 2004. *Dropout Rates in the United States: 2001* (NCES 2005-046). Washington, D.C.: U.S. Department of Education, National Center for Education Statistics. http://nces.ed.gov/pubs2005/2005046.pdf.

Kaufman, Phillip, Marilyn McMillen, and David Sweet. 1996. *A Comparison of High School Dropout Rates in 1982 and 1992*, NCES 96-893, October 1996, U.S. Department of Education, National Center for Education Statistics, Table 10.

Koretz, Dan and Mark Berends. 2001. *Changes in High School Grading Standards in Mathematics, 1982-1992.* Santa Monica, Calif.: RAND. http://www.rand.org/publications/MR/MR1445.

Miao, Jing and Walt Haney. 2004. *High School Graduation Rates: Alternative Methods and Implications.* Arizona State University: Education Policy Studies Laboratory. Education Policy Analysis Archives. Vol. 12, No. 55. http://epaa.asu.edu/epaa/v12n55/v12n55.pdf.

National Governors Association. 2005. *Graduation Counts: A report of the National Governors Association Task Force on State High School Graduation Data.*

Orfield, G. (editor). 2004. *Dropouts in America: Confronting the Graduation Rate Crisis.* Cambridge, Mass.: Harvard Education Press.

Orfield, G., D. Losen, J. Wald, and C. Swanson. 2004. *Losing Our Future: How MinorityYouth are Being Left Behind by the Graduation Rate Crisis.* Cambridge, Mass.: The Civil Rights Project at Harvard University.

Phelps, Richard P. 2005. *A Review of Greene (2002) High School Graduation Rates in the United States*, Practical Assessment, Research and Evaluation. Vol. 10, No. 15. http://pareonline.net/pdf/v10n15.pdf.

Rumberger, R.W. and S.P Lamb. 2003. The early employment and further education experiences of high school dropouts: A comparative study of the United States and Australia. *Economics of Education Review.* Vol. 22, pp. 353-66.

Sum, Andrew et al. 2003. *The Hidden Crisis in the High School DropoutProblems of Young Adults in the U.S.: Recent Trends in Overall School Dropout Rates and Gender Differences in Dropout Behavior.* Washington, D.C.: The Business Roundtable. http://www.businessroundtable.org/pdf/914.pdf.

Swanson, Christopher. 2003. *Keeping Count and Losing Count: Calculating Gradua-tion Rates for All Students Under NCLB Accountability*. Washington, D.C.: Education Policy Center, The Urban Institute.

Swanson, Christopher. 2004. *Who Graduates? Who Doesn't? A Statistical Portrait of Public High School Graduation, Class of 2001*. Washington, D.C.: The Urban Institute. http://www.urban.org/UploadedPDF/410934_WhoGraduates.pdf.

Tyler, John, Richard Murnane, and J. Willett. 2000. Estimating the labor market sig-naling value of the GED. *The Quarterly Journal of Economics*, Vol. 115, No. 2, pp. 431-68.

Tyler, John. 2004. Does the GED improve earnings? Estimates from a sample of both successful and unsuccessful GED candidates. *Industrial and Labor Relations Review*. Vol. 57, No. 4. pp. 579-98.

U.S. Bureau of the Census. 2002. *Design and Methodology*. Technical Paper 63RV. Current Population Survey. Washington, D.C.: U. S. Government Printing Office.

Warren, John R. 2005. *State-level High School Completion Rates: Concepts, Mea-sures, and Trends*. Arizona State University: Education Policy Studies Labora-tory. Education Policy Analysis Archives, Vol. 13, No. 51. http://epaa.asu.edu/epaa/v13n51.

Yates, Julie. 2005, The transition from school to work: education and work experi-ences. *Monthly Labor Review*. February. http://www.bls.gov/opub/mlr/2005/02/art4full.pdf.

Young, Beth Aronstamm. 2003. *Public High School Dropouts and Completers From the Common Core of Data: School Year 2000–01*. Washington, D.C.: U.S. De-partment of Education, National Center for Education Statistics. http://nces.ed.gov/pubs2004/2004310.pdf.

Zahs, Daniel, Steven Pedlow, Marjorie Morrissey, Patricia Marnell, and Bronwyn Nichols. 1995. *High School and Beyond Fourth Follow-Up Methodology Report*. U.S. Department of Education, National Center for Education Statistics.

About EPI

The Economic Policy Institute was founded in 1986 to widen the debate about policies to achieve healthy economic growth, prosperity, and opportunity.

In the United States today, inequality in wealth, wages, and income remains historically high. Expanding global competition, changes in the nature of work, and rapid technological advances are altering economic reality. Yet many of our policies, attitudes, and institutions are based on assumptions that no longer reflect real world conditions.

With the support of leaders from labor, business, and the foundation world, the Institute has sponsored research and public discussion of a wide variety of topics: trade and fiscal policies; trends in wages, incomes, and prices; education; the causes of the productivity slowdown; labor market problems; rural and urban policies; inflation; state-level economic development strategies; comparative international economic performance; and studies of the overall health of the U.S. manufacturing sector and of specific key industries.

The Institute works with a growing network of innovative economists and other social science researchers in universities and research centers in the U.S. and abroad who are willing to go beyond the conventional wisdom in considering strategies for public policy.

Founding scholars of the Institute include Jeff Faux, distinguished fellow and former president of EPI; Lester Thurow, Sloan School of Management, MIT; Ray Marshall, former U.S. secretary of labor, professor at the LBJ School of Public Affairs, University of Texas; Barry Bluestone, Northeastern University; Robert Reich, former U.S. secretary of labor; and Robert Kuttner, author, editor of *The American Prospect,* and columnist for *Business Week* and the Washington Post Writers Group.

For additional information about the Institute, contact EPI at 1333 H Street NW, Suite 300, Washington, D.C. 20005, (202) 775-8810, or visit www.epi.org.

DATE DUE
